WE MAKE PLAYING BASS A NO-BRAINER!

SINCE 1922

Alfred Music Publishing Co., Inc. • P.O. Box 10003 • Van Nuys, CA 91410-0003

alfred.com

ISBN-10: 0-7390-7112-2 (Book & DVD)
ISBN-13: 978-0-7390-7112-0 (Book & DVD)

Bass photos (left to right) courtesy of Fender Musical Instruments Corporation and Schecter Guitar Research • Beethoven bust photo courtesy of www.Statues.com

 Printed on 100% recycled paper.

CONTENTS

ABOUT THE AUTHORS

The Meeting of Great Minds
In order to enlighten you, we have gathered together a stellar group of authors who specialize in different facets of teaching bass. Every one of them has contributed knowledge to make playing bass a no-brainer. Here is a little information on each of them.

Chuck Archard
Chuck has been playing the bass since the early 1970s. He holds BME and MME degrees from Morehead State University. He is an accomplished bassist, composer and educator and his original works have played on all the major television networks and in 20 international markets. He has performed with many legendary artists both live and in the studio, and has appeared on more than 30 CDs.

Dan Bennett
Dan has been playing bass and other instruments for over 10 years. He received his Bachelor's in Music Performance, with special emphasis in Music Business, from the University of Massachusetts Lowell. Dan has played in groups with various styles such as progressive metal, hardcore, punk, pop-rock, indie/alt rock, jazz and more. He is the author of The Total Rock Bassist, published by the National Guitar Workshop and Alfred Music Publishing.

L. C. Harnsberger
L. C. Harnsberger studied music composition at the University of Southern California. Since finishing school, he has been composing and performing as well as writing best-selling instructional books. His Kid's Guitar Course (co-written with Ron Manus) has received numerous awards and continues to grow in popularity. Other publications include bass methods, guitar methods, reference books, and music for band and orchestra. He is currently the editor-in-chief of the Musical Instruments division at Alfred Music Publishing.

Paul Lidel
By the time Paul signed his first major-label recording contract at age 23, he had already been playing professionally since age 14. Paul has over 2,000 shows under his belt, having toured abroad and performing in 45 states in the U.S. Paul's latest project had him recording and performing with the band Dangerous Toys. In addition to performing, Paul also enjoys teaching guitar at the University of Texas and has been on the faculty of the National Guitar Workshop.

David Overthrow
David has been a bass performer and instructor for over 20 years. He studied at Berklee College of Music and later earned a Bachelor of Music degree from Western Connecticut State University. David performs regularly in New York City and Connecticut. In addition to appearing on several CDs in styles ranging from funk to rock to reggae, he records with his own band, HIPpOCKET.

Ron Manus
Ron is co-owner of Alfred Music Publishing and its sister company, Daisy Rock Guitars. He is one of Alfred Music's most prolific and top-selling authors, with over 100 published titles to his credit. Ron has written instructional books for guitar, bass, banjo, harmonica, and ukulele. In addition to holding prominent positions with Alfred and Daisy Rock, Ron also plays guitar and sings in the rock-solid, no-nonsense, punk rock band sASSafrASS.

PART 1: THE BASICS

PARTS OF THE BASS

VIDEO EXAMPLE

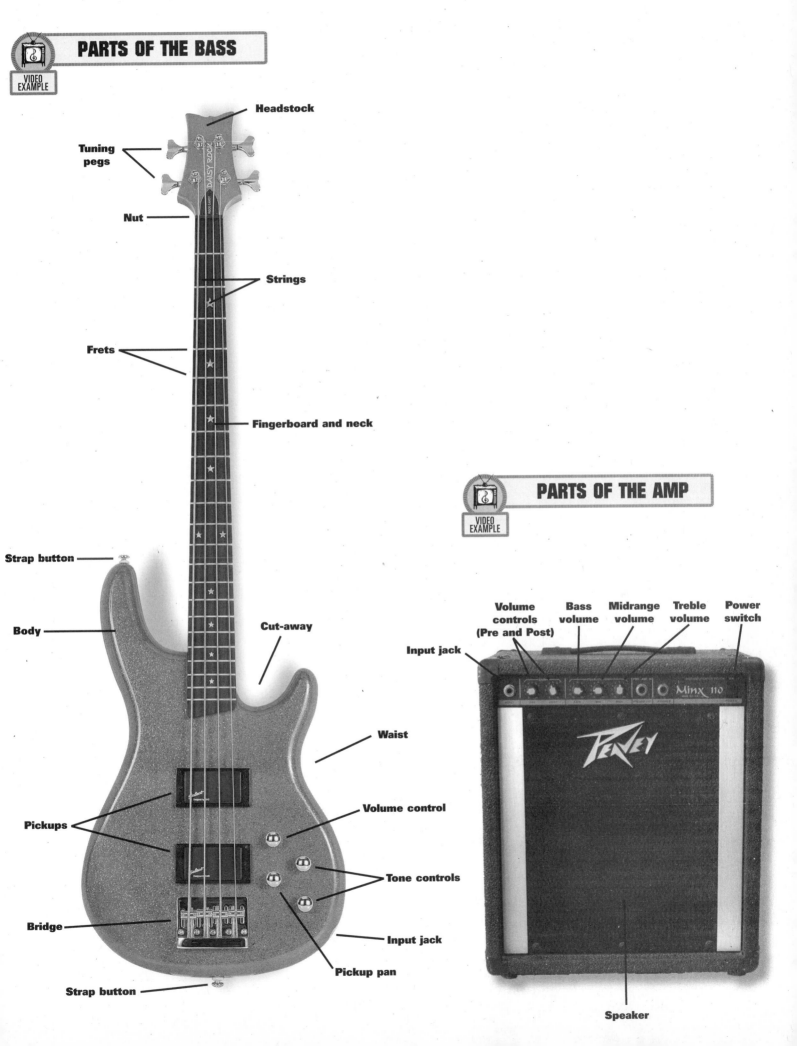

Headstock

Tuning pegs

Nut

Strings

Frets

Fingerboard and neck

Strap button

Body

Cut-away

Pickups

Waist

Volume control

Tone controls

Bridge

Input jack

Pickup pan

Strap button

PARTS OF THE AMP

VIDEO EXAMPLE

Volume controls (Pre and Post)

Bass volume

Midrange volume

Treble volume

Power switch

Input jack

Speaker

HOW TO HOLD YOUR BASS

Below are two ways to hold your bass.
Pick the one that is most comfortable for you.

Sitting.

Standing with strap.

THE RIGHT HAND

VIDEO
EXAMPLE

Proper Hand Position
There are two common ways of playing the strings. One is with your fingers, and the other is with a pick. Using your fingers may give you more speed and flexibility where playing with a pick will give you a very sharp attack and brighter sound.

Using Your Fingers
Most players alternate their index and middle fingers to pluck the strings. If you aren't comfortable using two fingers, start off using only one finger, and add the other later. When playing with your fingers, it is important to notice that after striking the string, the finger comes to a rest on the next string except when playing the fourth string, where the finger rests on the pickup.

Index finger

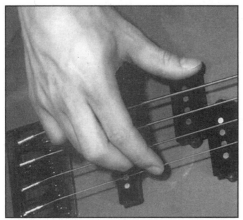

In position.

After striking the first string.

Middle finger

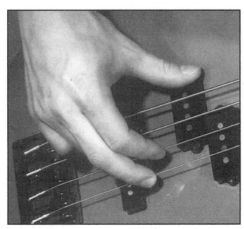

In position.

After striking the first string.

To get used to playing with the fingers, play a series of notes on an open string slowly and evenly. Do this with all four open strings.

GIVE IT
A TRY

Using a Pick

Hold the pick between your thumb and index finger. Hold it firmly, but don't squeeze it too hard.

To get used to playing with a pick, play a series of notes on an open string slowly and evenly. Do this with all four open strings.

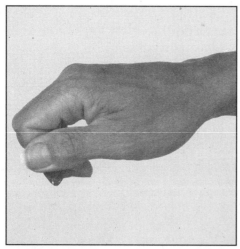

Holding the pick.

In position.

After striking the first string.

THE LEFT HAND

Proper Hand Position

Learning to use your left-hand fingers starts with a good hand position. Place your hand so your thumb rests comfortably in the middle of the back of the neck. Position your fingers on the front of the neck as if you are gently squeezing a ball between them and your thumb. Keep your elbow in and your fingers curved.

Keep your elbow in and fingers curved.

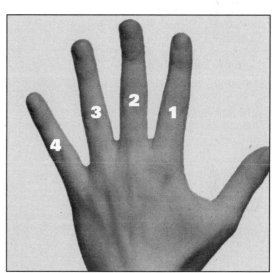

Numbers of the left-hand fingers.

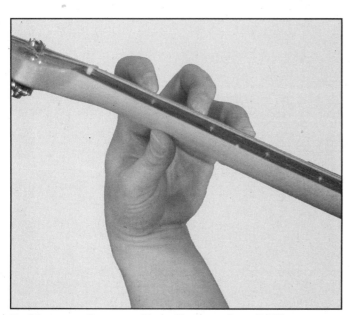

Position your fingers as if gently squeezing a ball between them and your thumb.

Placing a Finger on a String

When you press a string with a left-hand finger, make sure you press firmly with the tip of your finger and as close to the fret wire as you can without actually being right on it. Short fingernails are important! This will create a clean tone.

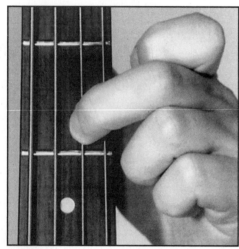

RIGHT
Finger is close to the fret without actually touching it.

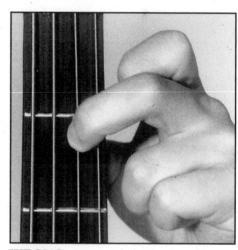

WRONG
Finger is too far from fret; sound is "buzzy" and unclear.

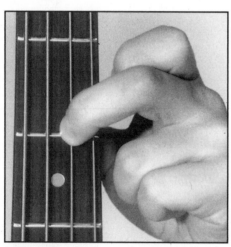

WRONG
Finger is on top of the fret; sound is muffled and unclear.

TUNING YOUR BASS

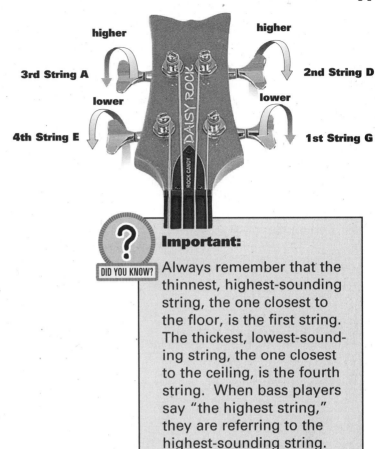

First, make sure your strings are wound properly around the tuning pegs. They should go from the inside to the outside as illustrated to the right.

Some basses have all four tuning pegs on the same side of the headstock. If this is the case, make sure all four strings are wound the same way, from the inside out.

Turning a tuning peg clockwise makes the pitch lower. Turning a tuning peg counter-clockwise makes the pitch higher. Be sure not to tune the strings too high because they could break.

Important:
Always remember that the thinnest, highest-sounding string, the one closest to the floor, is the first string. The thickest, lowest-sounding string, the one closest to the ceiling, is the fourth string. When bass players say "the highest string," they are referring to the highest-sounding string.

Using the CD

When tuning while listening to the CD, listen to the directions and match each of your strings to the corresponding pitches.

Tuning to a Piano or Keyboard

From lowest to highest, the bass is tuned to E, A, D, G, corresponding to the keys shown on the following diagram. The notes on the bass will sound an octave lower than the notes on the piano.

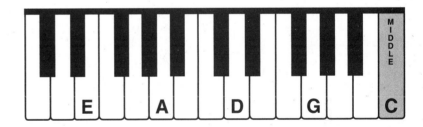

Tuning the Bass to Itself

When your fourth string is in tune, you can tune the rest of the strings using the bass alone. First, tune the fourth string to E on the piano. Then, follow the instructions below to get the bass in tune.

Press 5th fret of 4th string to get pitch of 3rd string (A).
Press 5th fret of 3rd string to get pitch of 2nd string (D).
Press 5th fret of 2nd string to get pitch of 1st string (G).

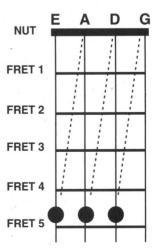

Pitch Pipes and Electronic Tuners

If you don't have a piano available, consider buying an electronic tuner or pitch pipe. There are many types available, and a salesperson at your local music store can help you decide which is best for you.

THE BASICS OF READING MUSIC

Musical sounds are indicated by symbols called notes.
Their time value is determined by their color (white or black)
and by stems or flags attached to the note.

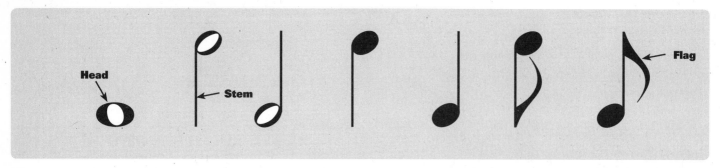

The Staff

The notes are named after the first seven letters of the alphabet (A–G), which are repeated
to embrace the entire range of musical sound. The name and pitch of a note are determined
by the note's position on five horizontal lines and four spaces between called the *staff*.

5th LINE

4th LINE

3rd LINE

2nd LINE

1st LINE

4th SPACE

3rd SPACE

2nd SPACE

1st SPACE

The Bass Clef

During the evolution of music notation, the staff had from 2 to 20
lines, and symbols were invented to locate a certain line and the
pitch of the note on that line. These symbols were called *clefs*.

Music for the bass is written in the *bass clef*. The symbol for the
bass clef is derived from the Old German way of writing the letter
F. Sometimes the bass clef is called the *F clef*, because the two dots
surround the 4th line of the staff to show it is the note F.

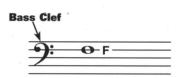

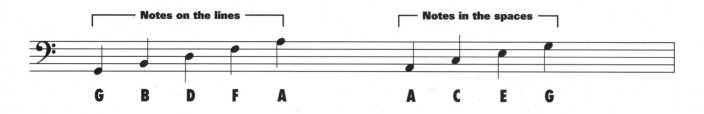

Notes on the lines

Notes in the spaces

G   B   D   F   A   A   C   E   G

You may want to use this simple trick to remember the notes.
On the lines: **G**reat **B**ig **D**ogs **F**ight **A**nimals.   On the spaces: **A**ll **C**ars **E**at **G**as.

Measures (Bars)

Music is also divided into equal parts
called *measures* or *bars*. One measure
is divided from another by a *bar line*:

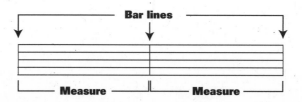

COUNTING TIME

Four Kinds of Notes

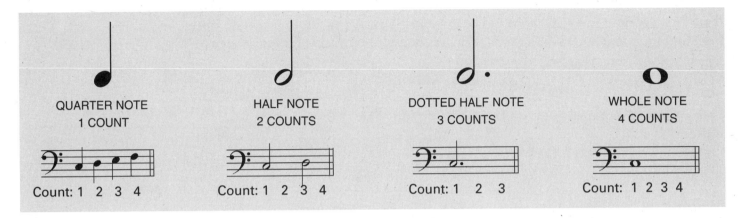

Time Signatures
Each piece of music has numbers at the beginning called a
time signature. These numbers tell us how to count time.

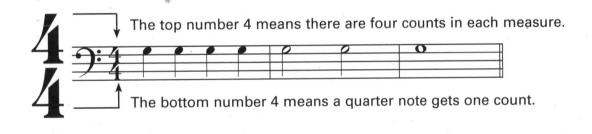

The top number 4 means there are four counts in each measure.

The bottom number 4 means a quarter note gets one count.

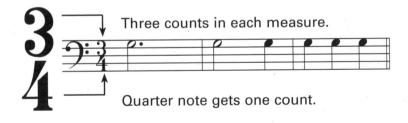

Three counts in each measure.

Quarter note gets one count.

All the music in this book is written two ways: in standard music notation and in *TAB*. Since most folios of popular music use TAB, it is important to know how to read TAB in addition to standard music notation. Always read the standard notation first, and then use the TAB as your guide to playing the music in the correct position.

Below each traditional music staff you'll find a four-line TAB staff. Each line represents a string of the bass, with the highest, thinest string at the top and the lowest, thickest string at the bottom.

T	1st string (G)
	2nd string (D)
A	3rd string (A)
B	4th string (E)

Numbers placed on the TAB lines tell you which fret to play. A zero means to play the string open (not fingered).

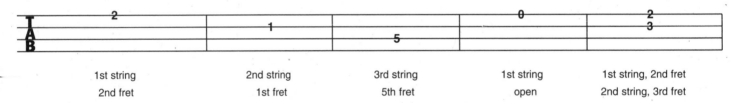

1st string	2nd string	3rd string	1st string	1st string, 2nd fret
2nd fret	1st fret	5th fret	open	2nd string, 3rd fret

By glancing at the TAB, you can immediately tell where to play a note. Although you can't tell exactly what the rhythm is from the TAB, the horizontal spacing of the numbers gives you a strong hint about how long or short the notes are to be played.

By glancing at the TAB, you can immediately tell where to play a note. Although you can't tell exactly what the rhythm is from the TAB, the horizontal spacing of the numbers gives you a strong hint about how long or short the notes are to be played.

NOTES ON THE FIRST STRING G

OPEN STRING
Finger: O (open)
G

2nd FRET
Finger: 2
A

A double bar line indicates the end of a piece.

Playing Quarter Notes

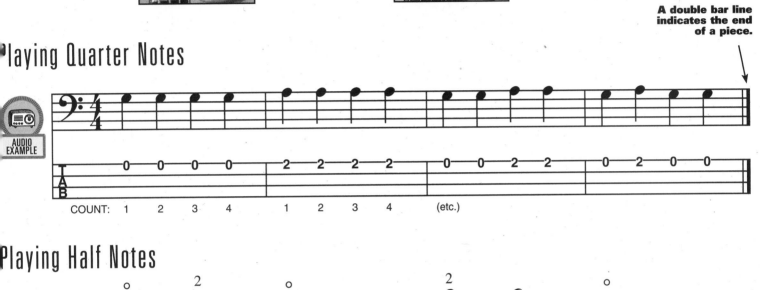

Playing Half Notes

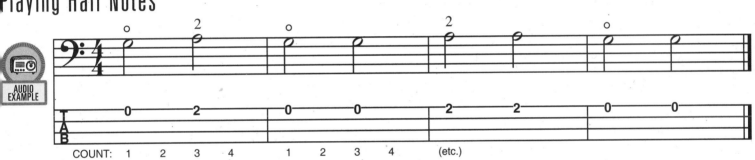

Playing Dotted Half Notes

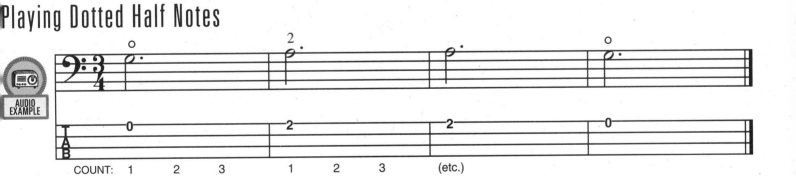

Playing Whole Notes

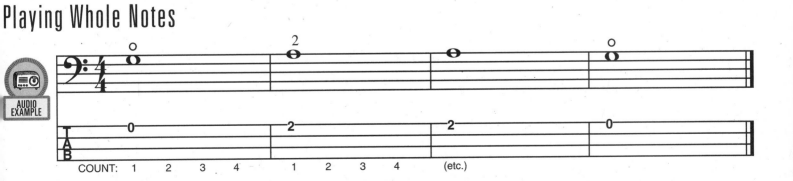

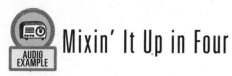

Mixin' It Up in Four

Continue to next line
without stopping.

COUNT: 1   2   3   4   (etc.)   1   2   3   4

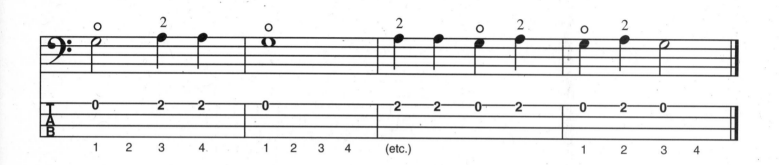

1   2   3   4.   1   2   3   4   (etc.)   1   2   3   4

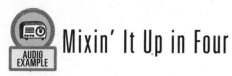

Mixin' It Up in Three

Continue to next line
without stopping.

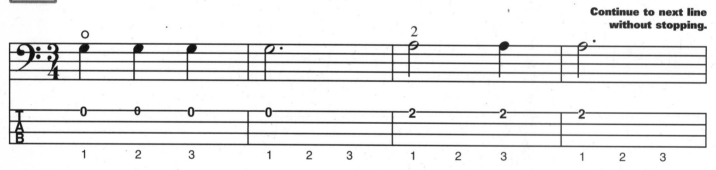

1   2   3   1   2   3   1   2   3   1   2   3

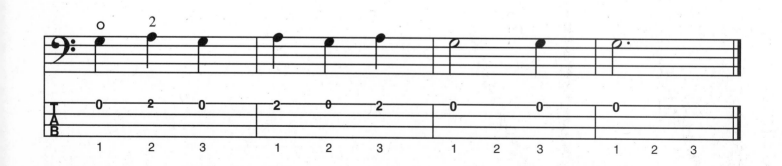

1   2   3   1   2   3   1   2   3   1   2   3

NOTES ON THE SECOND STRING D

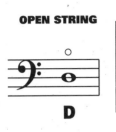

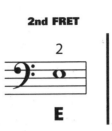
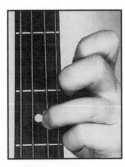

OPEN STRING — D
2nd FRET — 2 — E
3rd FRET — 3 — F

If you have trouble playing with the third finger alone, try adding the fourth finger until you build up strength in your third.

TIPS

Playing D, E and F

Once Again

Extra Credit in Three

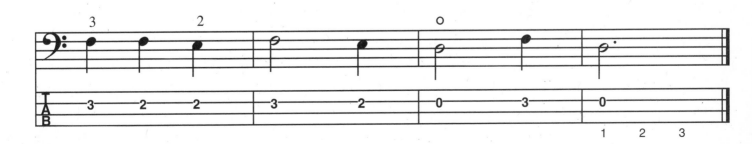

COMBINING NOTES ON THE G & D STRINGS

 ### Two-String Warm-up
Here is a great daily warm-up exercise that uses the notes you have learned so far.

 Chord symbols that are placed above each staff may be used for a duet. Have a friend or teacher play the chords on the guitar or keyboard while you play the bass line, or play along with the audio track on the CD or DVD. Many of the tunes in the rest of this book include chords for duets.

 ### D Minor Blues
Here is a great bass line to use when playing a D minor blues.

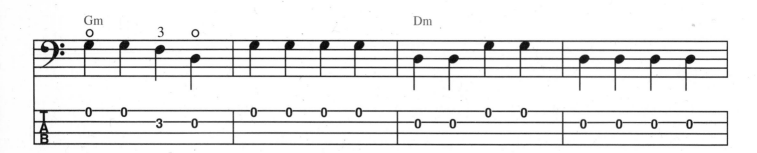

NOTES ON THE THIRD STRING A

   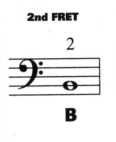 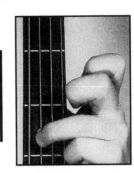 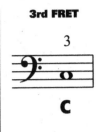

OPEN STRING — A
2nd FRET — 2 — B
3rd FRET — 3 — C

Up-Stems & Down-Stems

Until now, all notes have been written with the stems pointing down.
To make music look neater, down-stems *and* up-stems are used:

Notes above or on the middle line have stems pointing down.

Notes below the middle line have stems pointing up.

A Few New Notes

Lookin' Up

20

THE A NATURAL MINOR SCALE

A *scale* is a set of eight notes in alphabetical order arranged according to a specific pattern. Scales that follow the same pattern have a characteristic sound that is distinctly different than that of other types of scales.

The *natural minor scale* in A is also known as the *Aeolian mode*. This scale includes every note you've learned so far. Play it many times as part of a daily warm-up. Keep the beat steady and get a clean sound.

Rockin' à la Mode

SHARPS

A sharp sign ♯ placed before a note means to play that note one fret higher than usual. If the note is usually played on the open string, finger the sharp note on the 1st fret with the 1st finger.

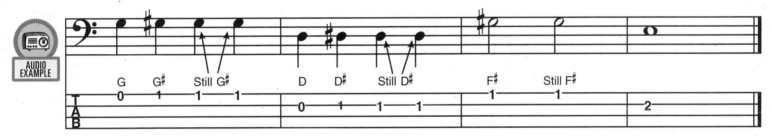

If the note is usually fingered, play the sharp note one fret higher.

Since the note E♯ is the same as F, it is not used much. The same goes for B♯, which is the same as C.

Sharp Example No. 1 A sharp stays in effect for a whole measure.

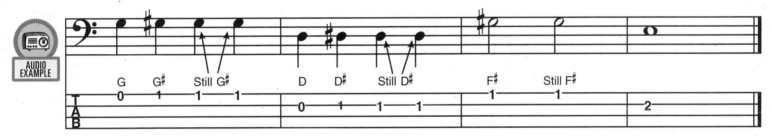

Sharp Example No. 2 The bar line restores a sharp note to its usual position.

NATURALS

A natural sign ♮ cancels a previous sharp sign in the same measure.

VIDEO EXAMPLE

NOTES ON THE FOURTH FRET

You can play notes on the 4th fret with your 4th finger, or, if you do not have enough finger strength at this time, you can shift your 3rd finger up to the 4th fret.

1st STRING, 4th FRET

3 or 4

B

2nd STRING, 4th FRET

3 or 4

F#

3rd STRING, 4th FRET

3 or 4

C#

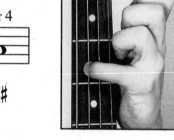

Practice these exercises that include notes on the 4th fret.

Fourth Finger Frenzy

Still F#

Little Finger Challenge

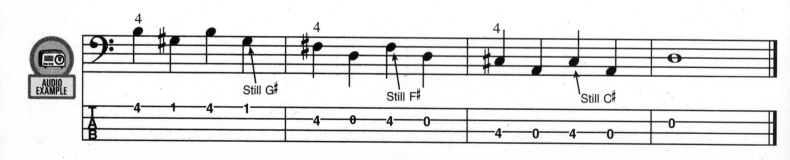

Still G#   Still F#   Still C#

NOTES ON THE FOURTH STRING E

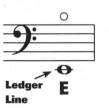

OPEN STRING

Ledger Line → **E**

1st FRET

1

F

2nd FRET

2

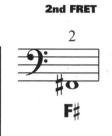

F#

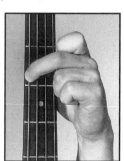

The short line that extends the staff downward for E is called a *ledger line.* On a standard bass, only the low E requires a ledger line below the staff.

3rd FRET

3

G

4th FRET

4

G#

 The E string is the largest string on the bass, which makes it the most difficult to play. Be sure to press very hard with the left hand, close to the fret (without being right on it).

E-String Strut

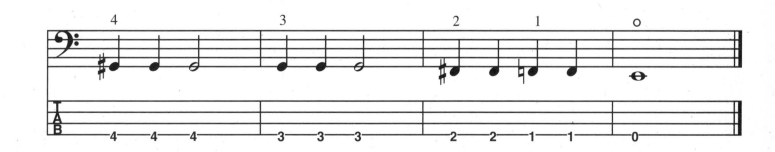

Note-Finding Review

The following exercise uses every note you've learned so far.
Practice it until you can play without missing a beat.

Swing Bass Line

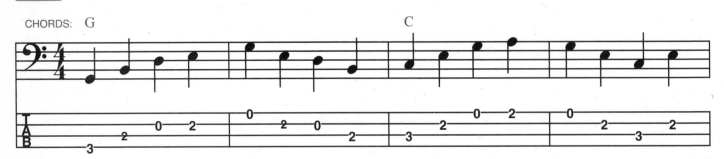

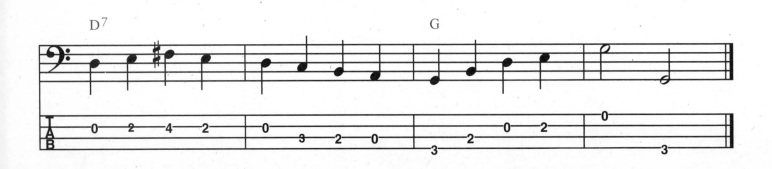

 **OCTAVES**

You've learned the notes E, F, F♯, G, G♯, and A on the G and D strings.
You've also learned the same notes on the A and E strings, but they sound lower.
Notes that have the same letter name but sound lower or higher are in a different *octave*.
An octave is a note eight notes from another note. Think of an octopus (eight arms)
or an octet (a group of eight musicians). Octaves are an important part of bass lines
in every style of music.

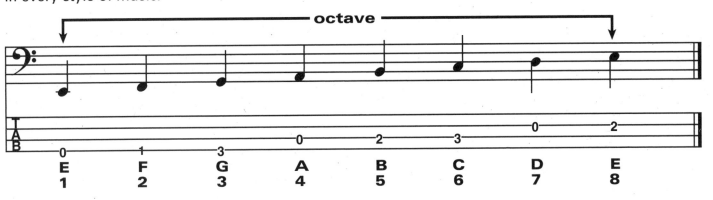

All the Octaves You Know So Far

26

Octabass 12

MetalOctavus

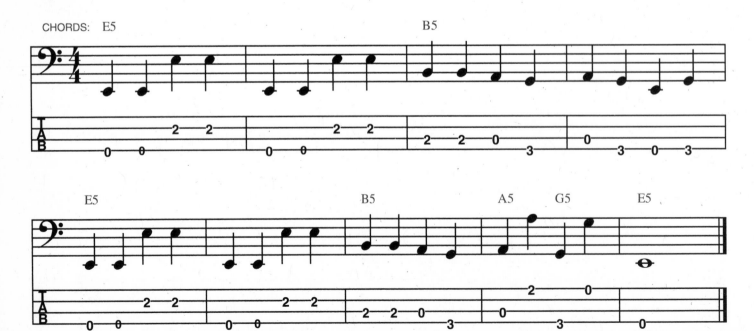

FLATS

A flat sign ♭ placed before a note means to play that note one fret lower than usual. For example, if the note is usually fingered at the 2nd fret, the flat note is played at the 1st fret; if the note is usually played at the 3rd fret, play the flat note at the 2nd fret.

To flat an open-string note, play the next-lower string at the 4th fret.

Jammin' with Sharps, Naturals & Flats

Just as for a sharp, a bar line restores a flatted note to its usual position.
A natural sign ♮ cancels a previous flat in the same measure.

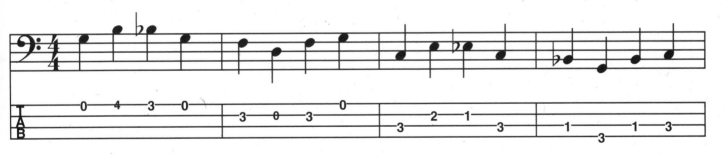

Practice the following exercises until you can play them without missing a beat.

Flats and Naturals

Flats, Sharps and Naturals

Bluesy Lick

 THE KEY OF F MAJOR

The F Major Scale

A *major scale* is a series of eight notes in a specific arrangement of *half steps* (next fret) and *whole steps* (skip a fret). The pattern is always **W W H W W W H** (W= whole step, H= half step). The F major scale begins on F and contains a B♭.

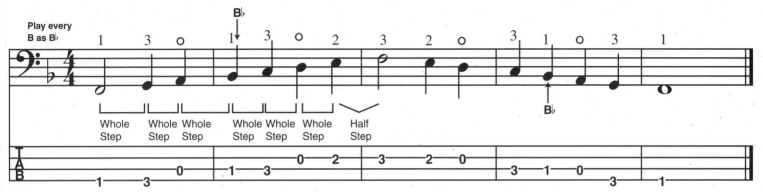

Key Signatures and Repeat Signs

Flats or sharps placed at the beginning of every staff line are known as a *key signature*. A key signature of one flat (B♭) means to play every B as a B♭, unless preceded by a natural sign. It also tells you the music is in the *key of F major*. A *key* is kind of a musical "home base" from which the music departs and eventually returns. Notice that pieces in the key of F almost always end on the note F.

The Extended F Major Scale

The following exercise extends the F major scale to the high B♭.

Rockin' in F

A repeat sign at the end of a piece means to go back to the beginning and play the entire piece again.

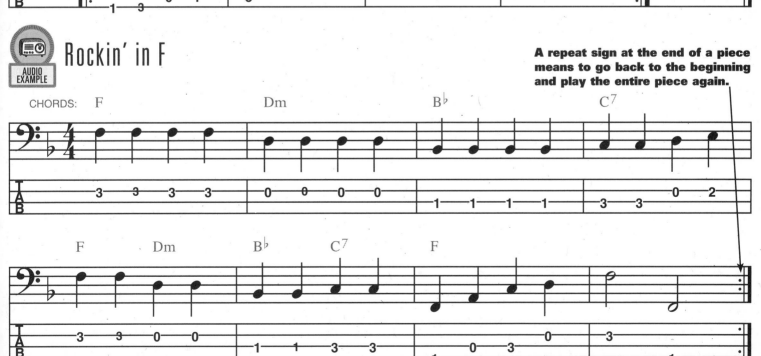

Funky Bass

Waltz in F

Rock Ballad in F

THE KEY OF B♭ MAJOR

A key signature of two flats (B♭ and E♭) tells you the piece is in the *key of B♭ major*.
Unless preceded by a natural sign, all B's are played as B♭'s and all E's are played as E♭'s.

First practice the scale, then play the exercise.

The B♭ Major Scale

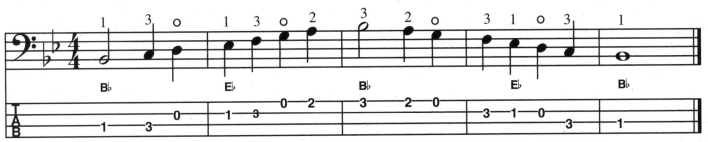

Jazz Blues in B♭

Flats, sharps and naturals that appear in a piece but do not belong to that key (such as E♮ and A♭ in this piece) are called *accidentals*.

B♭ Bass Line

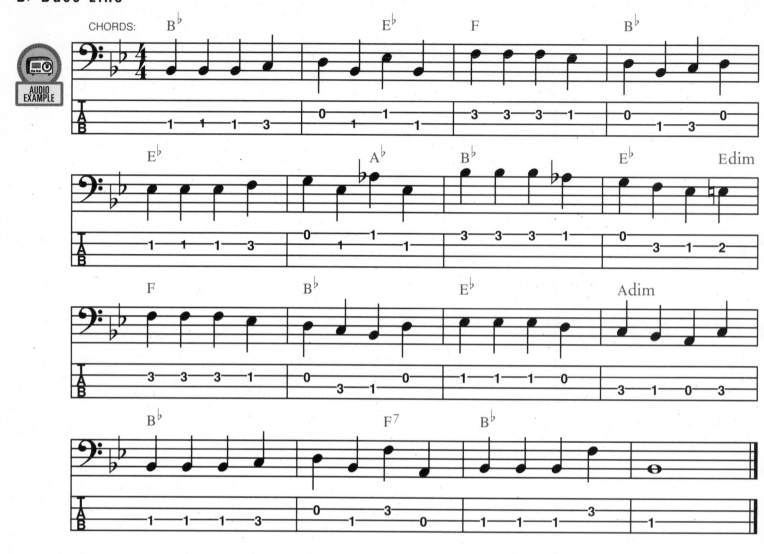

Hold On

THE CHROMATIC SCALE

VIDEO EXAMPLE

The *chromatic scale* is completely made up of half steps. When the chromatic scale is ascending, it is written with sharps; when it is descending, it is written with flats.

Ascending Chromatic Scale

Descending Chromatic Scale

Chromatic Rock

Bumble Bass

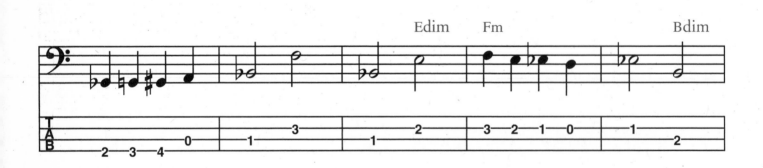

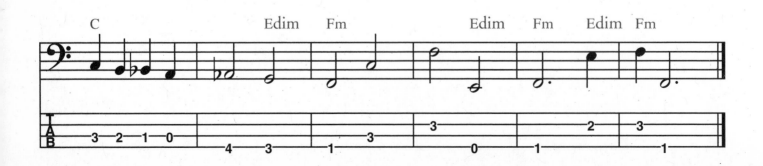

EIGHTH NOTES

Eighth notes are black notes with a flag added to the stem ♪ or ♩.
Two or more eighth notes are written with a beam connecting the stems:
There are two eighth notes per beat, and eight eighth notes per measure
in 4/4 time, which are counted **1 & 2 & 3 & 4 &.**

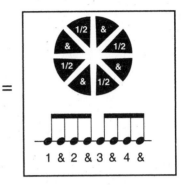

When playing eighth notes with your right hand, alternate between your index finger *i* and middle finger *m*.

Eighth Notes on an Open String

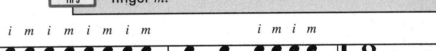

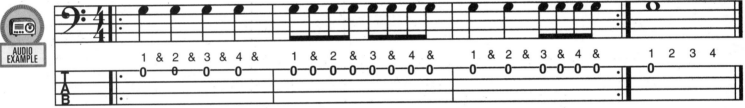

Eighth Notes on Three Open Strings

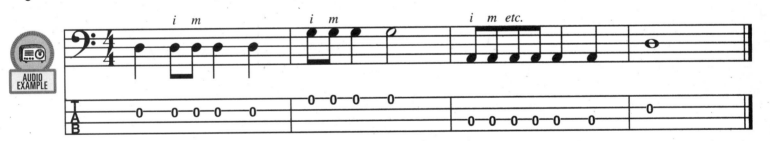

Eighth Notes with Fingered Notes

Quick Time

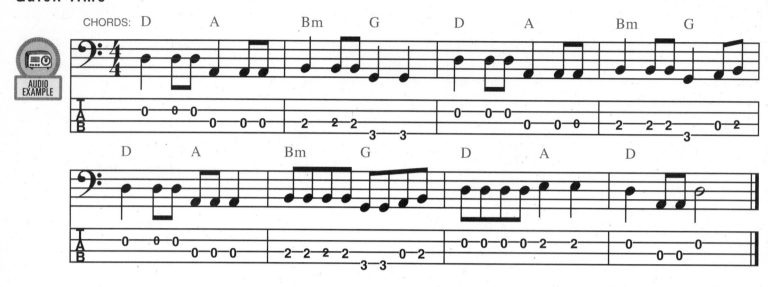

Early Rock with Eighths

> When you are fingerpicking and moving quickly from a higher string to a lower string, try using the same finger (*i* or *m*) to play both strings.

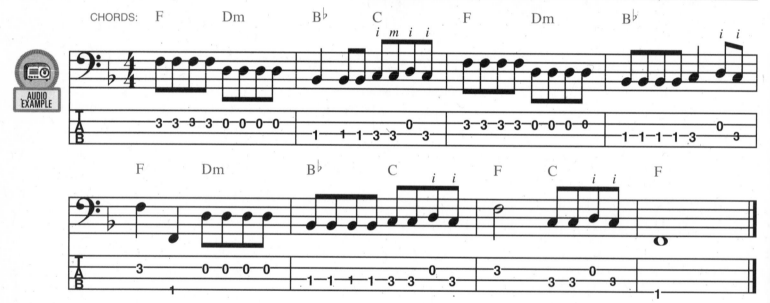

Eightude

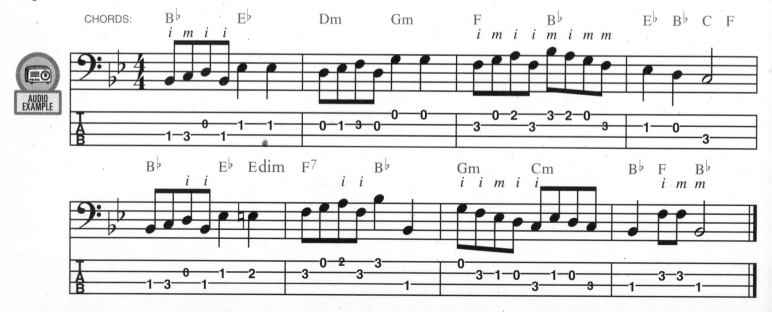

RESTS

In music, a *rest* is a measured silence. It is important to get a clean sound when playing rests.

If the note before a rest is open, stop the vibration of the string with the fingers of the left hand.

If the note is fingered, release the pressure on the string, but keep the finger touching it.

Three Basic Rests

QUARTER REST	HALF REST	WHOLE REST

One beat of silence.

Two beats of silence.

A whole measure of silence (four beats in $\frac{4}{4}$ time, three beats in $\frac{3}{4}$ time).

TIPS An easy way to remember the difference between the half rest and whole rest is to think of the whole rest as being longer, or "heavier," and so it hangs below the line. The half rest is shorter, or "lighter," and so it sits on top of the line.

Rest Exercise No. 1

Rest Exercise No. 2

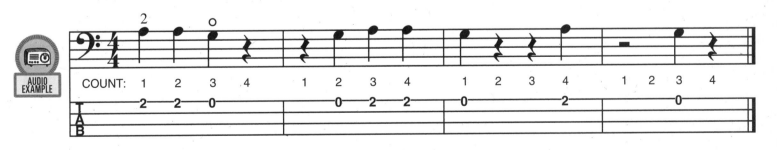

No Time to Rest

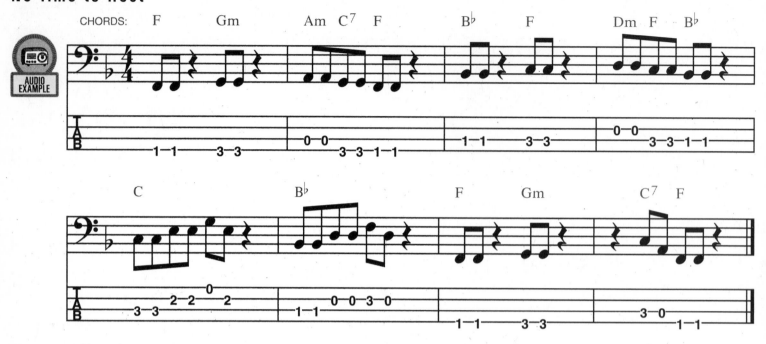

Quiet Time

WARM-UPS IN THE KEYS OF F & B♭

The following exercises in the keys of F and B♭ combine eighth notes with other rhythms and make use of most of the notes you've learned so far. Serious students will want to add this page to their daily warm-ups.

Warm-up in F

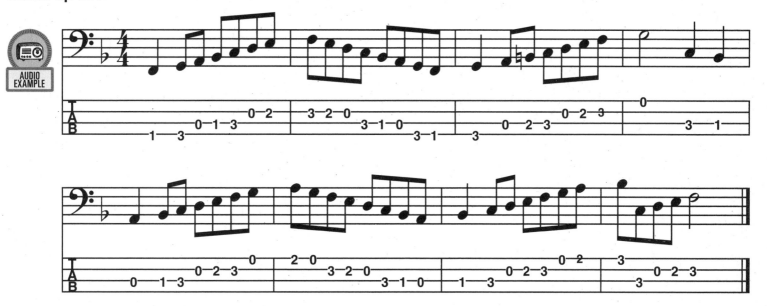

Warm-up in B♭ No. 1

Warm-up in B♭ No. 2

LICKS IN THE KEYS OF F & B♭

A *lick* is a short phrase, usually one or two measures long, that musicians use to fill in dead spots in the music and to add interest to their playing.

F Lick No. 1

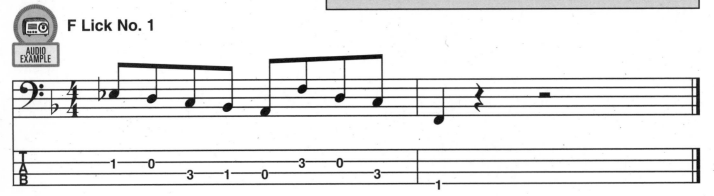

F Lick No. 2

B♭ Lick No. 1

B♭ Lick No. 2

SECOND POSITION

All the notes you have played so far have been in *first position*, which means your left hand fingers have been placed on the first four frets. The G major scale below is in *second position*. This means that the left hand is shifted up the fingerboard so that the 1st finger plays the notes on the 2nd fret, the 2nd finger plays the notes on the third fret, the 3rd finger plays the notes on the 4th fret, and the 4th finger plays the notes on the 5th fret.

THE KEY OF G MAJOR

The key signature of one sharp (F♯) tells you a piece is in the *key of G major*. All F's are played as F♯'s unless preceded by a natural sign.

The version of the G major scale below is in second position.

THIRD POSITION

When playing in *third position*, shift the left hand so the 1st finger plays notes on the 3rd fret, the 2nd finger plays notes on the 4th fret, and the 3rd finger plays notes on the 5th fret.

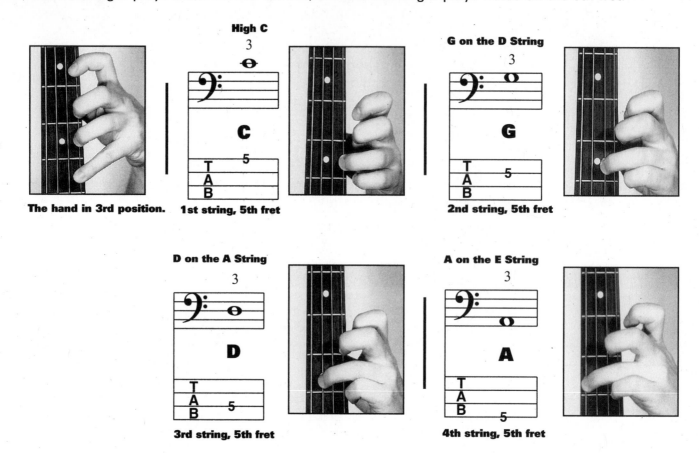

The hand in 3rd position.   1st string, 5th fret   2nd string, 5th fret

3rd string, 5th fret   4th string, 5th fret

Notice that you now have alternate ways of playing the notes G, D, and A. Compare the following:

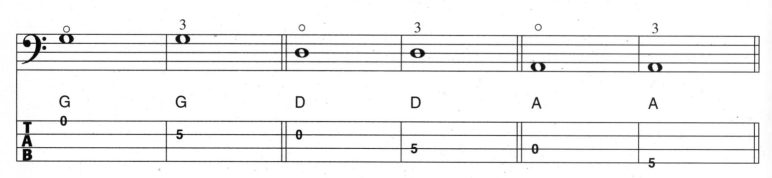

It is impossible to give a hard and fast rule about whether to use the open or fingered form of a note. Many players avoid using open strings altogether, but the best policy is to try a passage both ways and choose the form that is easier to play and produces the better sound.

For example, for the following passage, most players would find the fingering in the first measure easier to play.

THE KEY OF C MAJOR

A key signature with no sharps or flats tells you a piece is in the *key of C major*. All notes are played natural unless preceded by a sharp or flat.

First practice the scale, then the exercises. The fingering for some notes will change depending on your hand position.

The C Major Scale

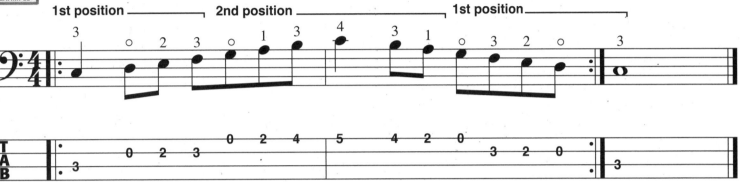

Warm-up in C

Bass Line for a Rocker

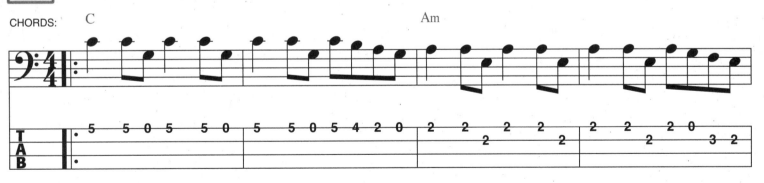

44

THE SLIDE

Slide

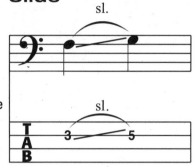

To play a slide from a note to a higher note, pick the first note, then slide the fret finger up to sound the higher note without picking again.

Slide Up

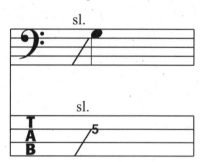

To slide up to a note, play the string as your fret hand slides up the neck to the written pitch.

Below are some examples of slides used in country bass licks.

Slide Example No. 1

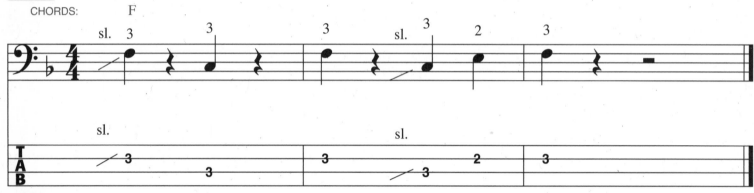

Slide Example No. 2

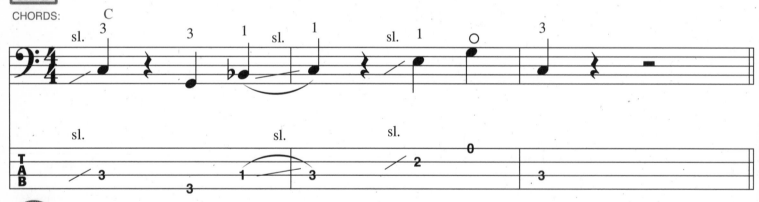

Slide Example No. 3

ACCENTED NOTES

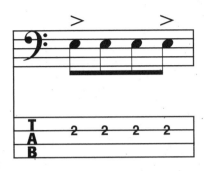

An *accent* (>) means to play a note slightly louder than usual. The picking hand plucks the string harder for an accented note than for non-accented notes.

Below are examples of accented notes used in rock bass licks.

Accent Example No. 1

Accent Example No. 2

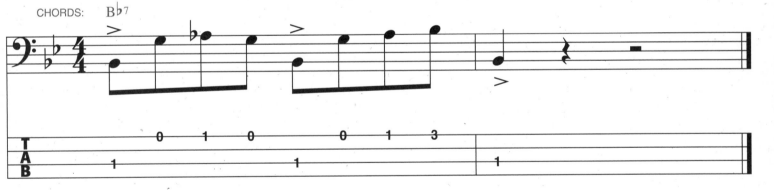

Accent Example No. 3

TIES & SYNCOPATION

Ties

Ties are curved lines connecting two or more successive notes of the same pitch. When two notes are tied, the second one is not picked, but its time value is added to the value of the first note. In TAB notation, a tied note is *sometimes* indicated with parentheses—do not pick that note again.

Syncopation

Syncopation is a musical effect in which a note is *anticipated*, meaning it's played before its expected beat. Syncopation is critical to all types of music.

Example 1 below is not a syncopated rhythm. Each quarter note falls in the expected place, right on the beat. Examples 2–6 are various examples of syncopation.

Example No. 1
Non-syncopated or "straight" version of the rhythm.

Example No. 2
Beat 3 anticipated. (The third quarter note is played early, on the "&" of beat 2 rather than its expected place on beat 3.)

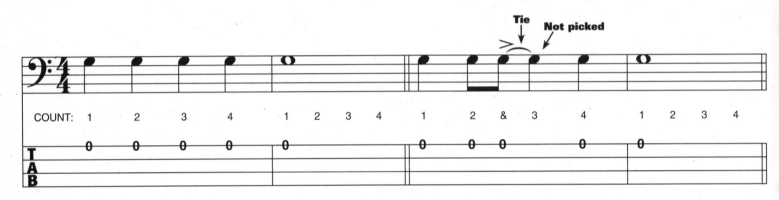

Example No. 3
Beat 1 anticipated across the bar line.

Example No. 4
Beat 2 anticipated.

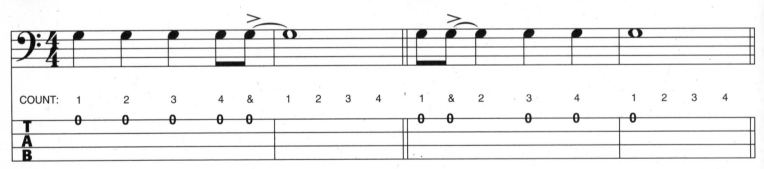

Example No. 5
Beats 2 and 3 anticipated.

Example No. 6
Beats 2, 3, and 4 anticipated.

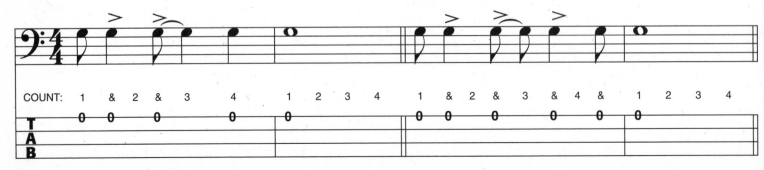

SYNCOPATION IN THE KEYS OF C, G, F & B♭

Remember to count carefully and accent all the anticipated notes.

Syncopation Example in C

Syncopation Example in G

Syncopation Example in F

Syncopation Example in B♭

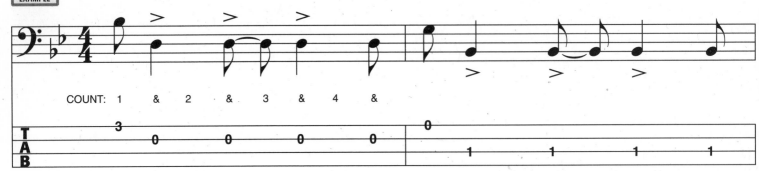

COUNT: 1 & 2 & 3 & 4 &

Syncopated Writing

CHORDS: C5

F5

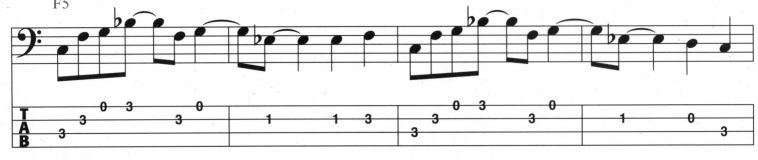

C5

THE DOTTED QUARTER NOTE

A dot to the right of a note increases its length by half. A dotted half note is equal to a half note tied to a quarter note for a total of three beats. A dotted quarter note equals a quarter note tied to an eighth note, which equals one and a half beats.

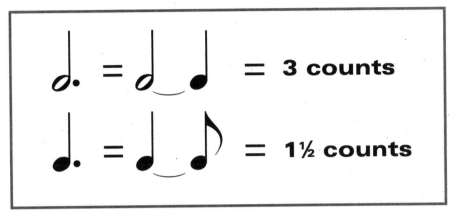

Preparatory Drill

This measure sounds the same as . . . . . this measure.

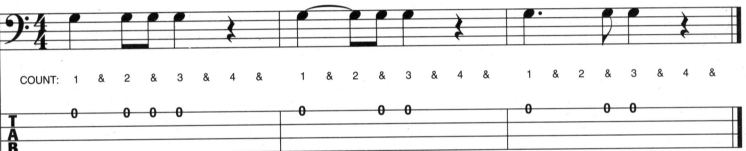

Rock Bass Line in G

Rock Bass Line in F

50

COMBINING DOTTED QUARTER NOTES, ACCENTS & SLIDES

ROCK LICKS WITH SYNCOPATION

Rock Lick in C No. 1

CHORDS: C

Rock Lick in B♭

CHORDS: B♭

Rock Lick in F

CHORDS: F

Rock Lick in C No. 2

CHORDS: C

HIGH C♯ (or D♭) AND D

These notes further extend the upper range of notes you've learned so far. The fingering of these notes will vary depending upon the context of the music.

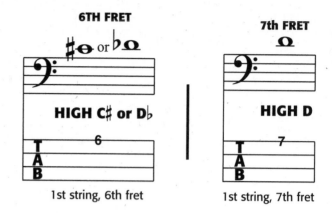

6TH FRET

HIGH C♯ or D♭

1st string, 6th fret

7th FRET

HIGH D

1st string, 7th fret

Exercise with High C♯ and D

Exercise with High D♭

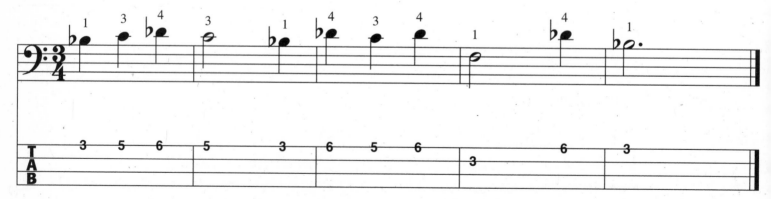

THE KEY OF D MAJOR

The key signature of two sharps (F♯ and C♯) tells you a piece is in the *key of D major*.
All F's are played as F♯'s and all C's are played as C♯'s, unless preceded by a natural sign.

The D Major Scale

Joy to the World

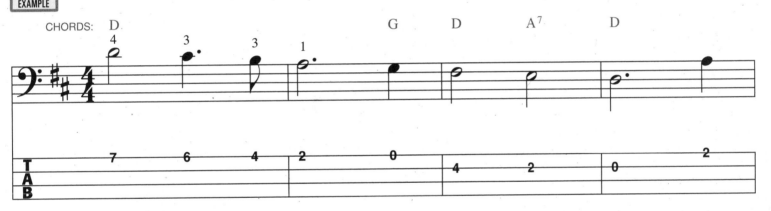

The D Scale in Repeated Notes

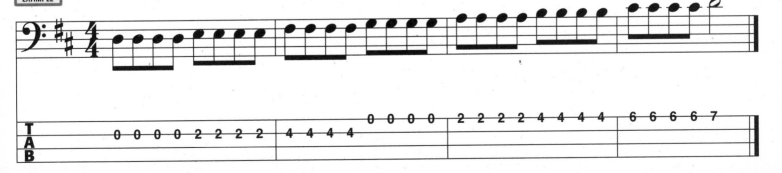

ROCK LICKS IN THE KEYS OF G, C & D

Rock Lick in G No. 1

Rock Lick in G No. 2

Rock Lick in C

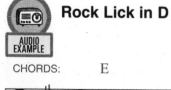

Rock Lick in D

HEAVY METAL LICKS IN G, C & D

Heavy Metal Lick in G No. 1

Heavy Metal Lick in G No. 2

TIPS: When moving up and down the neck and changing strings, it is sometimes easier to use the 4th finger to play notes usually played with the 3rd.

Heavy Metal Lick in C

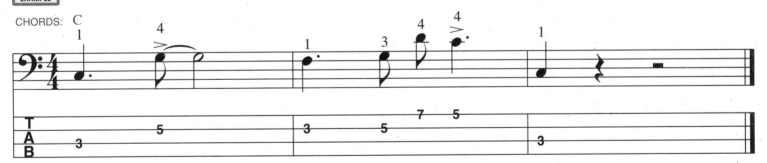

Heavy Metal Lick in D

SIXTEENTH NOTES & THE DOTTED 8TH AND 16TH NOTE RHYTHM

Sixteenth Notes

A *sixteenth note* is a black note with two flags added to the stem:

Two or more sixteenth notes are written with connecting stems:

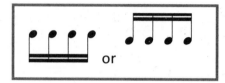

Sixteenth notes are played four to a beat, twice as fast
as eighth notes and four times as fast as quarter notes.

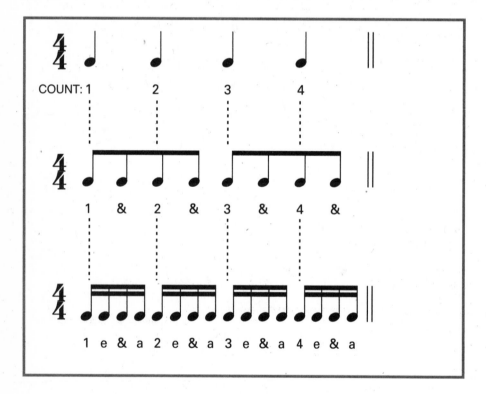

Dotted 8th and 16th Note Rhythm

The dotted 8th and 16th note rhythm is played in the time of one beat:

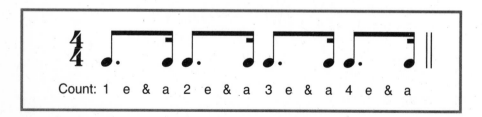

The dotted 8th and 16th note rhythm is used in many 1950s rock tunes and some blues. This rhythm is often called a *shuffle*. Practice the two examples below until you are comfortable with the feel.

Shuffle No. 1

Shuffle No. 2

SHUFFLE RHYTHM BASS LINES

Blues in C

Jazzy Bass Line in D

Rockin' Line in F

Cashin' In

CHORDS: Am

THE KEY OF A MAJOR

A key signature of three sharps (F♯, C♯, and G♯) tells you a piece is in the *key of A major*. All F's are played as F♯'s, all C's are played as C♯'s, and all G's are played as G♯'s, unless preceded by a natural sign. The key of A is very popular in rock and country music because it is an especially good-sounding key on the guitar.

The A Major Scale

Incomplete Measures

Not every piece of music begins on beat 1. Music sometimes begins with an incomplete measure called a *pickup*. If the pickup is one beat, the last measure of the piece will often have three beats if it's in 4/4 time, and two beats if it's in 3/4 time.

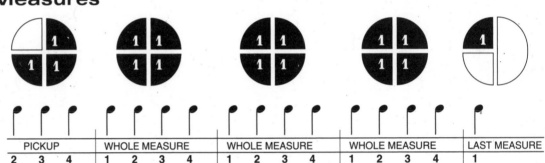

Bass Line for a Country Song

D.C. stands for *da capo*, Italian words that literally mean "from the head." It means to repeat the entire piece from the beginning. Notice that this example begins on beat 2 of the measure. Since the last measure has only one beat, it combines with the three beats in the first measure to make one complete bar of 4/4 time.

LICKS IN THE KEY OF A

Bass Lick in A No. 1

Bass Lick in A No. 2

Bass Lick in A No. 3

Bass Lick in A No. 4

THE KEY OF E MAJOR

A key signature of four sharps (F♯, C♯, G♯ and D♯) tells you a piece is in the *key of E major.* All F's are played as F♯'s, C's are played as C♯'s, G's are played as G♯'s, and D's are played as D♯'s, unless preceded by a natural sign.

Like the key of A, the key of E is very important in rock, blues and country music because it sounds good on the guitar.

The E Major Scale

E Major Warm-up in 4/4

E Major Warm-up in 3/4

HIGH D♯ (or E♭) AND E

These notes will extend your upper register even further.

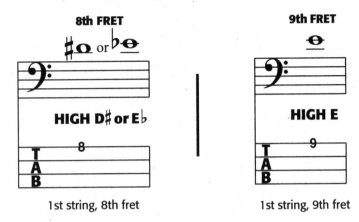

As with the notes learned on page 52, fingering depends on what precedes and what follows the note in question.

Exercise with High D♯ and E

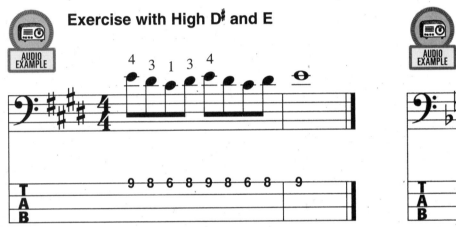

Exercise with High E♭

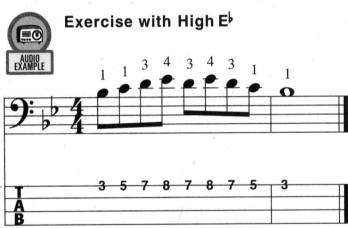

The Two-Octave E Major Scale

Your knowledge of the notes high D♯ and E allows you to play an E major scale in two octaves. Add this scale to your daily practice.

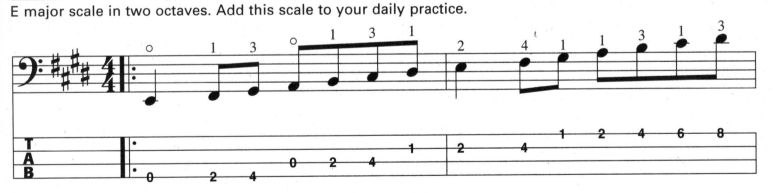

LICKS IN THE KEY OF E

E Major Lick No. 1

PHOTO BY JOE SIA/COURTESY OF STAR FILE PHOTO, INC.

DID YOU KNOW?

Victor Wooten *(b. 1964) is one of the foremost virtuoso bassists of his generation. Born into a musical family, he was playing gigs by age five with the Wooten Brothers Band. In 1988, he joined Béla Fleck and the Flecktones, along with his brother Roy "Future Man" Wooten. Victor soon became well-known in the bass community and beyond for the ease with which he performed the intricate compositions of the Flecktones. Their unique music defies classification, drawing from jazz, bluegrass, funk, and beyond. Wooten is widely regarded as a technical innovator who revolutionized the slap & pop technique. He continues to collaborate with Béla Fleck and also performs as a solo artist and with his brothers.*

PART 2: MORE ADVANCED PLAYING

Now that you have the basics under your fingers, let's move on to some more advanced concepts.

INTRODUCING TRIPLETS

A *triplet* is a group of three notes played in the time of two. For example, two eighth notes are played in one beat; three eighth notes with a *3* over or under them are called an *eighth note triplet*; they are played faster than eighth notes so that the three notes are played in the time of two regular eighth notes. You can remember the sound of eighth note triplets by saying the words "mer-ri-ly, mer-ri-ly." Each word sounds like an eighth note.

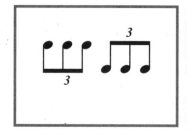

The exercises below contrast eighth note triplets with other rhythms.

 Triplet Test

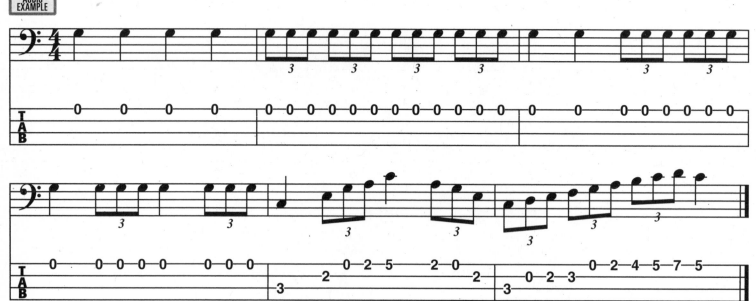

 Doo-Wop Triplets

 In the early days of rock, a type of ballad developed that depended on the triplet rhythm. Called "doo-wop," they are played slowly with a steady flow of triplets, as in this example.

Slowly

BASS LICKS WITH TRIPLETS

TRIPLET BASS LINES

Don't Trip

Triplet Time

Triplet and Two

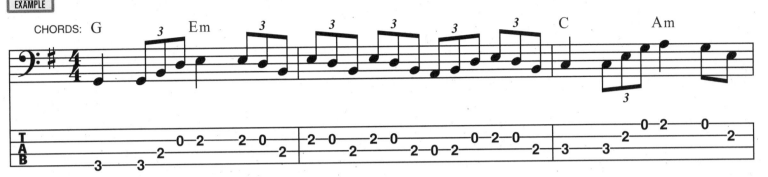

Trip-O-Meter

INTRODUCING $\frac{6}{8}$ AND $\frac{12}{8}$ TIME

The Time Signature $\frac{6}{8}$

6 = six beats in each measure
8 = eighth note gets one beat

In $\frac{6}{8}$ time, you usually group the measure into two groups of three.

The Time Signature $\frac{12}{8}$

12 = twelve beats in each measure
8 = eighth note gets one beat

In $\frac{12}{8}$ time, you usually group the measure into four groups of three. It has the same feel as a $\frac{4}{4}$ measure with four groups of eighth note triplets.

The Irish Washerwoman

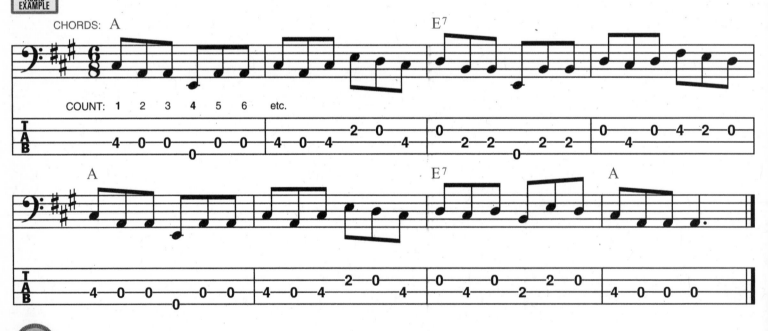

$\frac{12}{8}$ Rock Ballad

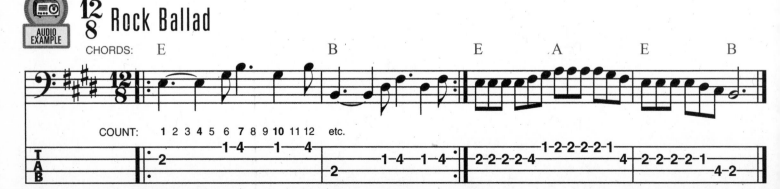

The quarter-eighth rhtyhm in this tune is sometimes called "swing feel." Swing feel is often used in blues and jazz styles and is also notated in $\frac{4}{4}$ time as two eighth notes or dotted-eighth and a sixteenth. Eighth notes played in swing style are called *swing eithths.*

Blues Shuffle in F

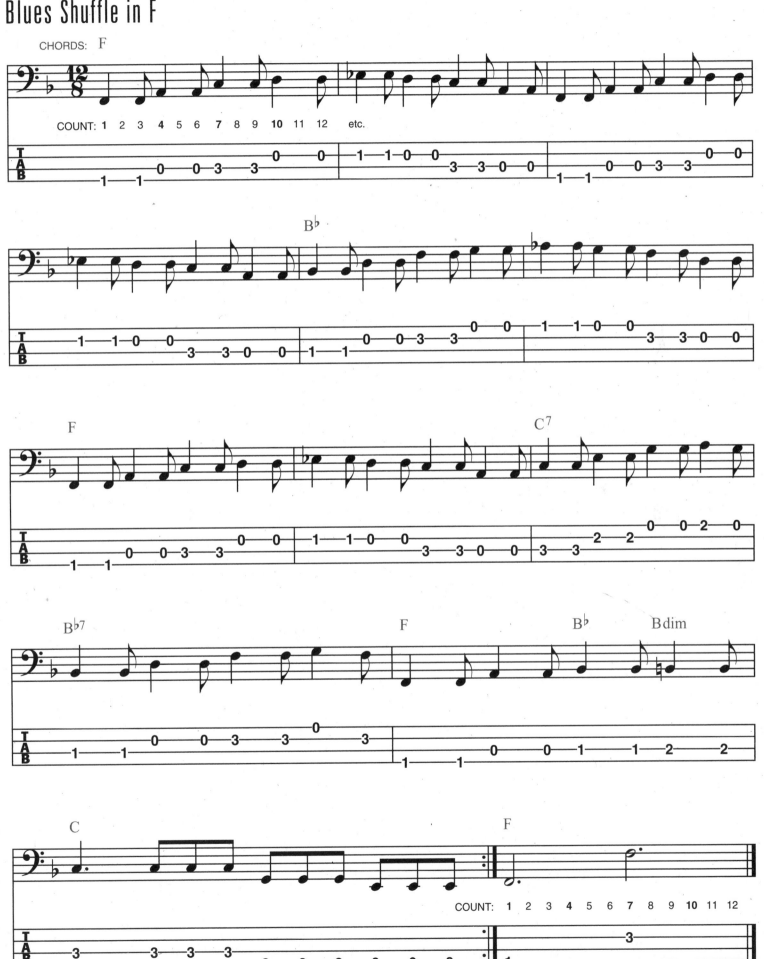

INTRODUCING CHORDS

Often, a bass player needs to play from a lead sheet. As a bass player, you are expected to create an effective bass line based on just the chords.

A *chord* is a group of three or more notes that are played at the same time. The three most common chords are *major chords*, *minor chords*, and *seventh chords*. Each of these types of chords is made up of a different pattern of note intervals. An *interval* is the distance from one note to another.

Major Chords

To find the notes of a C major chord, you need to use the C major scale. In the following C major scale, the interval number of each note is given below it. The first note, C, is the *root* (R) of the chord. The root is the most important note of a chord, and the note that names the chord; for example, C is the root of the C major chord, and D is the root of the D major chord.

C Major Scale

        R   2nd   3rd   4th   5th   6th   7th   R

The three intervals that make up a major chord are the root, third, and fifth. For a C major chord, those notes are C, E, and G.

C Major Chord

        R   3   5

Minor Chords

The easiest way to find the notes of a minor chord is to take a major chord and lower the third one half step (one fret). If the third of a major chord is a sharp note, make that note natural to make it a minor chord. The notes of a C minor chord are C, E♭, and G.

C Minor Chord

        R   ♭3   5

Seventh Chords

The most common seventh chord is called a *dominant seventh chord*. The dominant seventh chord is made up of the root, third, fifth, and seventh notes of the scale. For a C dominant seventh chord, use the same root, third, and fifth of the C major chord. Notice that the seventh note of the scale is B. To make a dominant seventh chord, you need to lower the seventh one half step to B♭.

C⁷ Chord

        R   3   5   ♭7

CHORD SYMBOLS

Each type of chord uses different symbols. The symbol for a major chord is a capital letter, like C, G, F♯, or E♭. If you see "E♭" on a lead sheet, it means to play an E♭ major chord.

The symbol for a minor chord is a small "m" following the note of the chord, such as Cm, Gm, F♯m, or E♭m. When you see "Cm" on a lead sheet, it means to play a C minor chord.

The symbol for a seventh chord is a capital letter followed by the number 7, such as G7, D7, F♯7, or E♭7.

The chart below shows you the notes of every common major, minor, and dominant seventh chord. (For a more complete chart of chords, see page 219.) Take the time to memorize this chart, since you will need to know all these chords to play bass lines.

Major Chords

	Root	3rd	5th
A =	A	C♯	E
B♭ =	B♭	D	F
B =	B	D♯	F♯
C =	C	E	G
D =	D	F♯	A
E♭ =	E♭	G	B♭
E =	E	G♯	B
F =	F	A	C
G =	G	B	D

Minor Chords

	Root	3rd	5th
Am =	A	C	E
B♭m =	B♭	D♭	F
Bm =	B	D	F♯
Cm =	C	E♭	G
Dm =	D	F	A
E♭m =	E♭	G♭	B♭
Em =	E	G	B
Fm =	F	A♭	C
Gm =	G	B♭	D

Seventh Chords

	Root	3rd	5th	7th
A7 =	A	C♯	E	G
B♭7 =	B♭	D	F	A♭
B7 =	B	D♯	F♯	A
C7 =	C	E	G	B♭
D7 =	D	F♯	A	C
E♭7 =	E♭	G	B♭	D♭
E7 =	E	G♯	B	D
F7 =	F	A	C	E♭
G7 =	G	B	D	F

PLAYING FROM LEAD SHEETS USING ROOTS

Here is a typical 1950s rock progression:

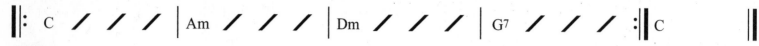

Example No. 1 The simplest thing you can do is play each root as a whole note. Even this simple device can be effective on the right song, say a doo-wop ballad like the Platters' 1955 hit, "Only You."

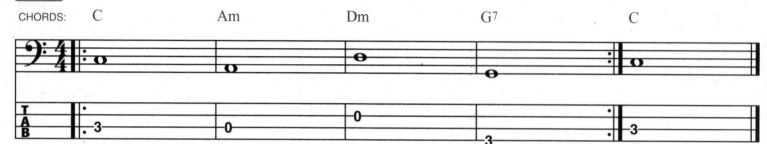

Example No. 2 On a bright rhythm tune like "Why Must I Be a Teenager in Love," half notes can be very effective.

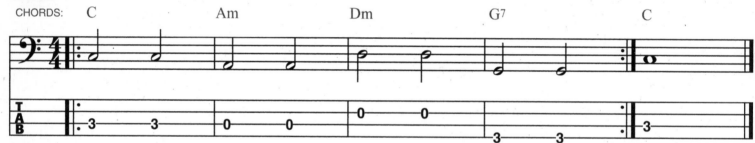

Example No. 3 Many early Motown hits by The Supremes and other groups featured bass lines in quarter notes, all on the root. Play this with a strong rhythmic drive.

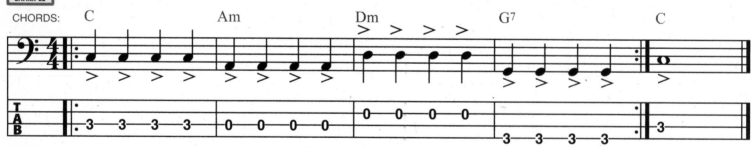

Example No. 4 This example should be played at a fairly quick tempo. It mixes various rhythms but uses only roots. Note the use of octaves in the fourth measure. Octaves are a great way to vary a bass line that uses repeated roots.

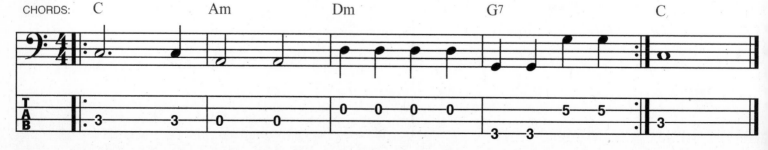

Many rock hits have been made by picking a catchy rhythm and repeating it throughout the song. Here are some examples of this technique, still limiting ourselves to playing roots.

Example No. 5
The dotted quarter/eighth note rhythm is characteristic of many rock styles.

Example No. 6
A variation on example No. 5.

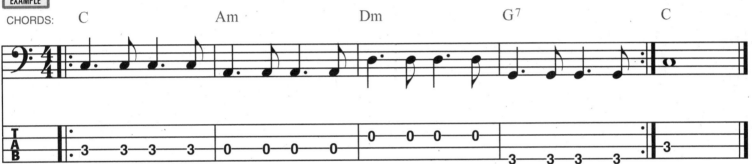

Example No. 7
A typical syncopated bass figure.

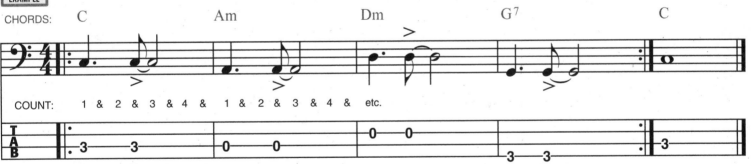

Example No. 8
A more complicated syncopation.

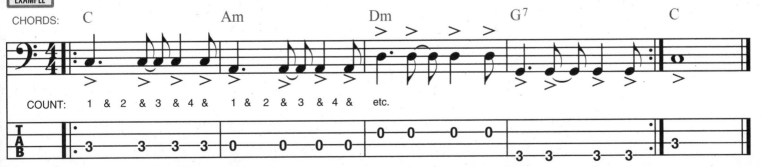

CREATE YOUR OWN BASS LINES USING ROOTS

Now that you know how to create bass lines using roots, here are some chord progressions in other keys. Make up your own bass lines using the ideas from pages 74 and 75.

Bass Line in G

CHORDS: G   Em   Am   D⁷   G

Bass Line in D

CHORDS: D   Bm   G   A⁷   D

Bass Line in A

CHORDS: A   D   A   E⁷   A

Bass Line in E

CHORDS: E   A   E   B⁷   E

A cool way to try out new bass lines is to get a guitar or keyboard player to play the chord progressions along with you.

GIVE IT
A TRY

Write your own bass lines. Start with a progression you like, and then fill in the root notes with rhythms you want. Pay attention to your time signatures,($\frac{4}{4}$, $\frac{6}{8}$, etc.), and make sure you have the right amounts of beats in each measure.

THE EIGHTH REST

This symbol ⅞ stands for ½ beat of silence. You can think of it as an unplayed eighth note. First, play measure 1, straight eighth notes. Then, play the variations on it, substituting a half beat of silence for each eighth rest. After an open note, place your left-hand fingers on the string to stop its vibration. After a fingered note, release the pressure on the string, but keep the fingers in contact with it to stop its vibration.

Example No. 1

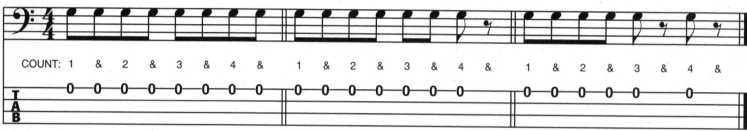

Example No. 2

Example No. 3

Explaining the Rest

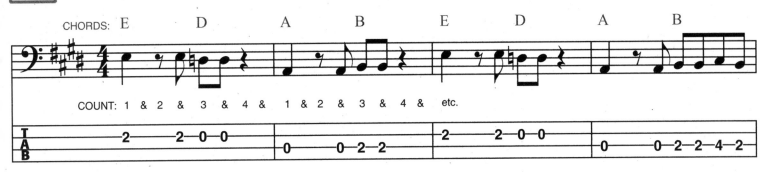

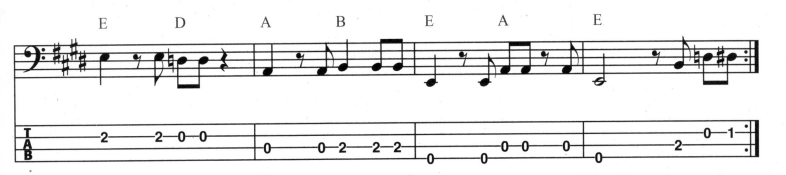

Jumpy Rests

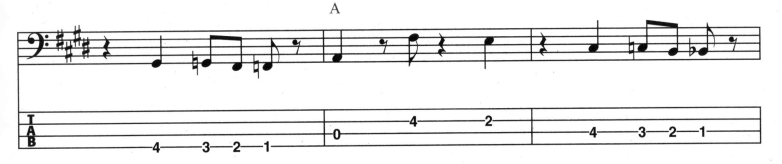

HIGH F

Knowledge of the high F allows you to extend your range to a full two-octave scale in the key of F.

Fingering will depend on what precedes and follows the F.

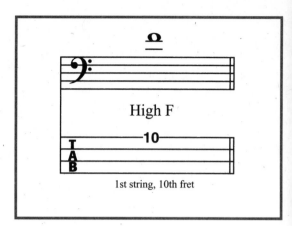

High F

1st string, 10th fret

The Two-Octave F Major Scale

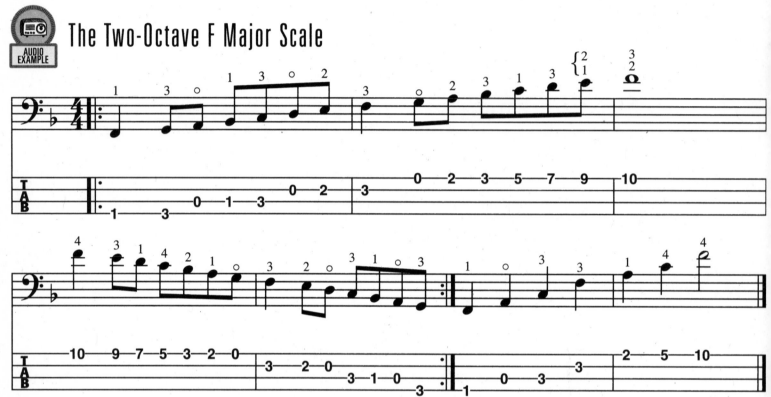

Study with High F

The sign ⅟ is called a *repeat sign*. It means to repeat the previous measure note for note. In the example below, the first measure is played a total of three times. Although the repeat sign is rarely seen in printed music, it is very common in hand-written manuscripts, so every musician should be familiar with it.

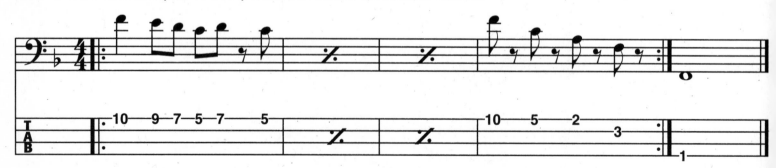

BASS LICKS IN F MAJOR

Lick No. 1

Moderately

CHORDS: F

Lick No. 2

Moderately

CHORDS: F

Lick No. 3

Moderately fast

CHORDS: F

Lick No. 4

Fast

CHORDS: F

Twistin'

Rushing Around

 ## Generations

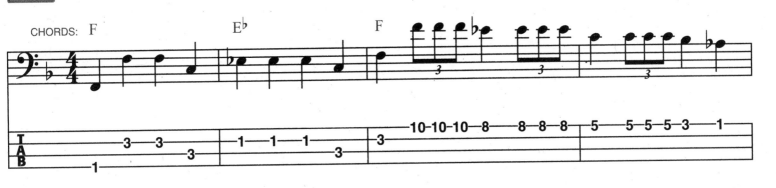

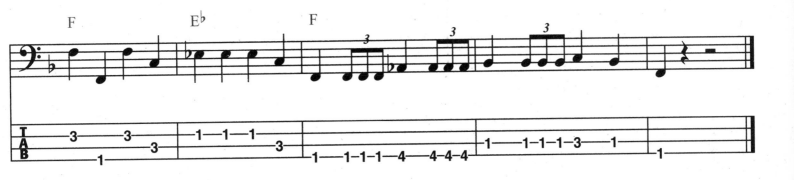

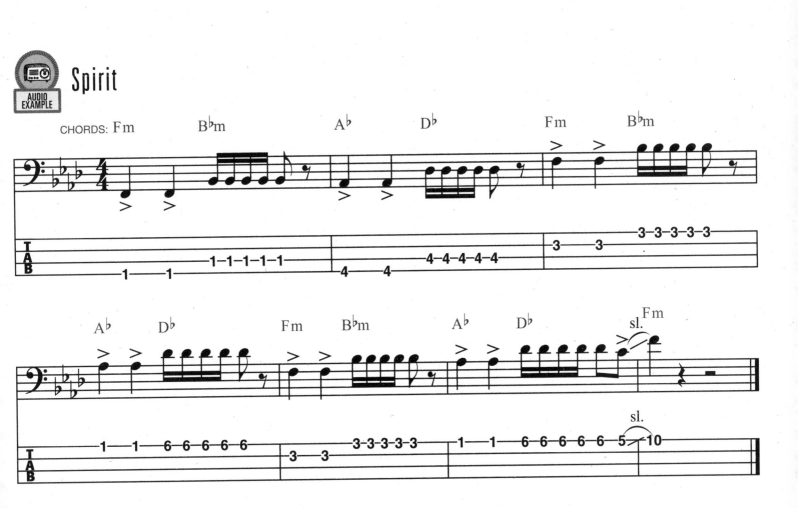
Spirit

CREATING BASS LINES USING ROOT–THIRD–FIFTH

Here are some typical bass lines based on common chord progressions. These bass lines all use the root, third, and fifth of each chord. Notice that the root has the most prominent place in the measure—the first beat. By keeping the root on the first beat, it is always very clear what chord is being played. Keep aware of the notes you are playing and whether they are the root, third, or fifth of the chord. By knowing these patterns, you will be able to play these licks for any chord.

 In quarter notes.

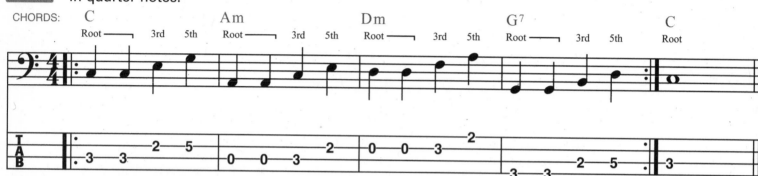

 Adding eighth notes adds drive to the bass line.

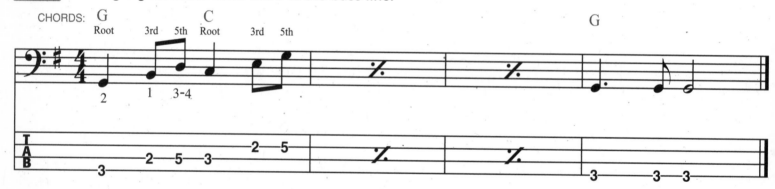

 Sometimes you will want to mix the notes up. In this case, R–third–fifth–third works great to create a 1950s-style bass line.

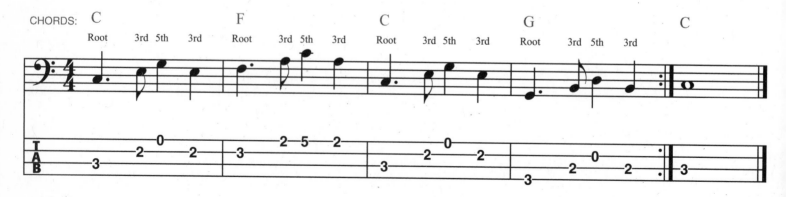

Any chord tone can be approached by a *lower neighbor* note (LN) a half step (one fret) below.

Any chord tone can be approached by an *upper neighbor* note (UN) a half or whole step (one or two frets) above.

You can combine upper and lower neighbor tones in the same bass line.

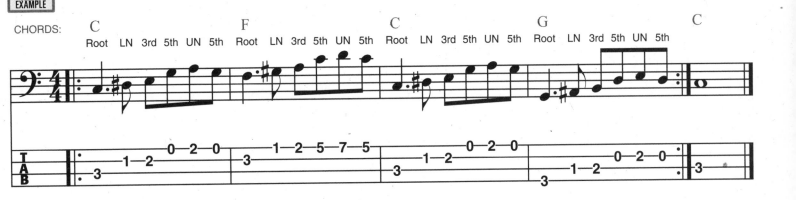

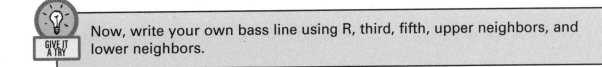

Now, write your own bass line using R, third, fifth, upper neighbors, and lower neighbors.

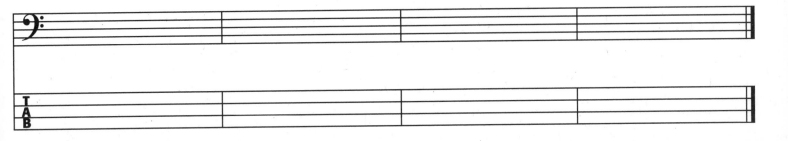

SHAPES OF R—3—5 ON THE FRETBOARD

As you create more bass lines, you'll notice certain patterns on the neck of the bass. The same patterns can be used for different chords as you go up and down the neck.

Let's look at the shape for a major triad. To see it clearly, we need to get familiar with the bass neck diagram. This diagram shows all the strings of the bass going vertically and the frets of the neck horizontally.

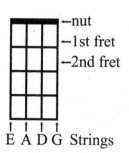

Black dots show what fret to finger on which string. When a note is played open, a circle is placed above the diagram over the appropriate string. The following example shows to play the open E string and the note B on the 2nd fret of the A string.

Here is the shape of an E major triad (R–3–5) starting with the open E string. This uses the E and A strings.

You can use this same shape to play the R, third, and fifth of an A triad and a D triad. The A triad is the same shape as the E triad, but played on the A and D strings. The D triad is played on the D and G strings.

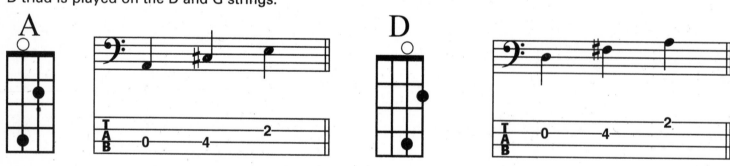

Here are the shapes when the root is on the 1st fret. In each case, the third is always an open string.

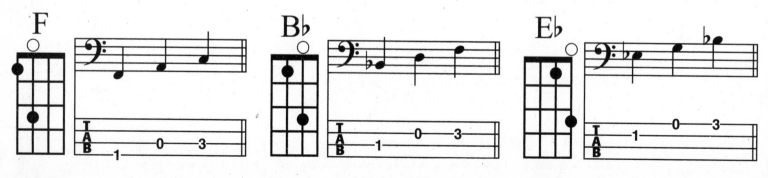

When the root is on the 2nd fret, there are no open strings.

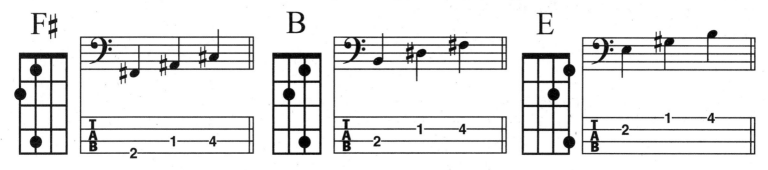

These shapes without any open notes are *transposable*, which means they can be moved up and down the neck and still have the same pattern of notes; in this case R, 3, 5. Here are the same shapes used for different chords.

88

MINOR R–♭3–5 SHAPES

Here is the shape of E minor, A minor, and D minor triads (R–♭3–5) starting with open strings

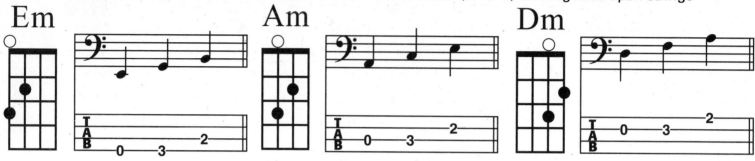

When the root is on the 1st fret, there are no open strings.

These shapes are transposable so you can move them up and down the neck and still have the same pattern of notes; in this case R, ♭3, 5. Here are the same shapes used for different chords.

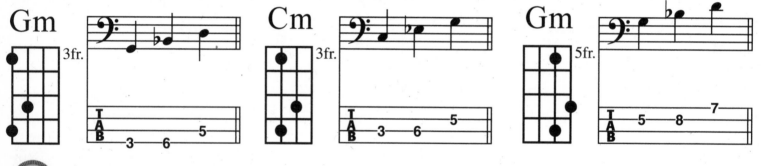

Shapely in Minor

Shaping Up

"Shaping Up" uses both major and minor transposable shapes.

Minor Funk

Chromatic Shapes

THE I–VI–IV–V PROGRESSION

Sometimes Roman numerals are used to refer to chords. Here is a review of some Roman numerals.

I = 1	IV = 4
II = 2	V = 5
III = 3	VI = 6
VII = 7	

The Roman numerals tell you the scale step that the chord is built on. For example, in the key of C, the **I** chord is a C chord (because the first note in the C scale is a C). In the key of F, the **I** chord is an F chord; in the key of D, the **I** chord is a D chord, and so on.

I   II   III   IV   V   VI   VII

The **VI** chord is a minor chord built on the sixth scale step. For example, the **VI** in C is an A minor chord.

The **IV** chord is a mojor chord built on the fourth scale step. For example, in the key of C, the **IV** chord is an F major chord.

The **V** chord is a major chord built on the fifth scale step. For example, in the key of B♭, the **V** chord is an F major chord.

This chart shows you the I, VI, IV, and V chords in all the commonly used keys:

Key	I Chord	VI Chord	IV Chord	V Chord
E	E	C♯m	A	B
A	A	F♯m	D	E
D	D	Bm	G	A
G	G	Em	C	D
C	C	Am	F	G
F	F	Dm	B♭	C
B♭	B♭	Gm	E♭	F

DID YOU KNOW? The I–VI–IV–V progression has been used in countless songs, in styles from swing to rock. Every bass player needs to be familiar with this progression in at least the keys shown above.

Here is an example of a simple **I–VI–IV–V** progression.

Using the **I–VI–IV–V** progressions from the chart on page 90, make up your own bass lines. Below, write out those you like best.

DYNAMICS

Signs that show how soft or loud to play are called *dynamics*. The most common dynamics are shown here:

p   stands for *piano* and means to play soft.

mf   stands for *mezzo forte* and means to play moderately loud.

f   stands for *forte* and means to play loud.

ff   stands for *fortissimo* and means to play very loud.

DID YOU KNOW? It is one thing to play all the right notes and rhythms, but the best musicians will vary the dynamics of a song to make the music really exciting.

Dynamic Blues

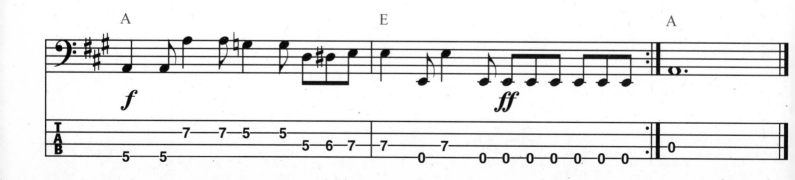

Dynamo

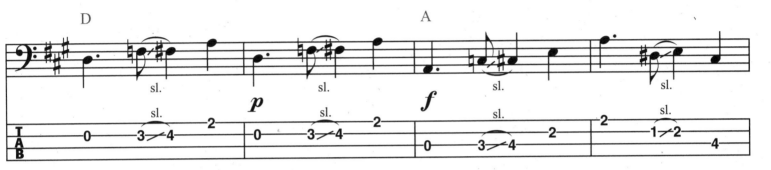

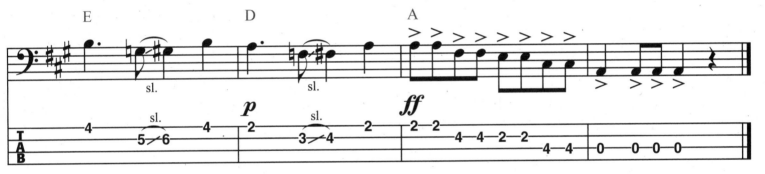

Dynam-ite

In "Dynam-ite," you start off piano and increase your dynamics to fortissimo. Even though the music is almost the same throughout, by increasing the dynamics, the music gets more and more exciting.

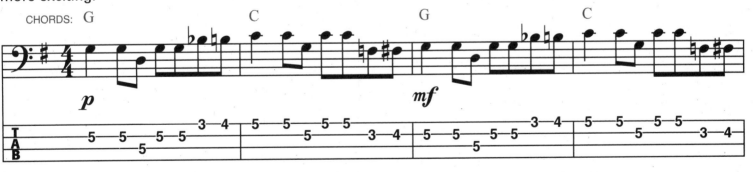

HIGH F♯ & G

The G note above high C is a very important note, as it lies an *octave* above the open G string. All bass guitars have the octave to the open strings marked in some distinctive way, usually with a double mother-of-pearl dot or diamond shape. The octave is at the 12th fret, and it may be easier for you to find that note and count backwards, back down the fingerboard.

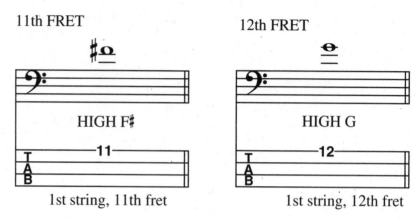

11th FRET   12th FRET

HIGH F♯   HIGH G

1st string, 11th fret   1st string, 12th fret

Knowledge of the high F♯ and G notes allows you to play a full two-octave G scale.

G Scale in Two Octaves

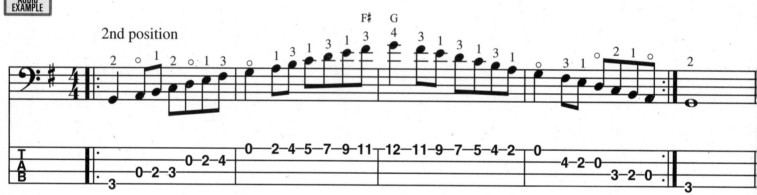

Chromatic Scale

This chromatic scale uses every note in the first octave of the G string.

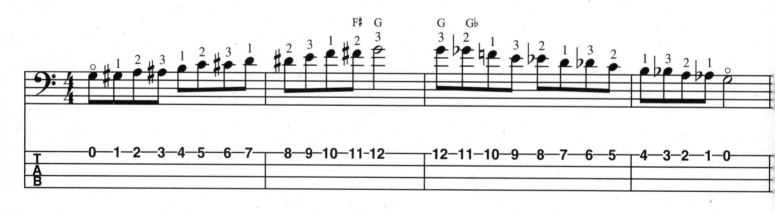

G MAJOR LICKS AND EXERCISES

Lick No. 1

Lick No. 2

G Major Exercise with High F# and G

INTRODUCING THE STACCATO

A small dot placed above or below a note is called a *staccato*. To play a note staccato means to play that note shorter than the normal note value, like there is a very short rest between the stacatto note and the following beat. Play the note like you normally would, but release the pressure on the string with your left hand just before the next note or rest.

 Jam Man

Cowboy Jazz

Stayin' in California

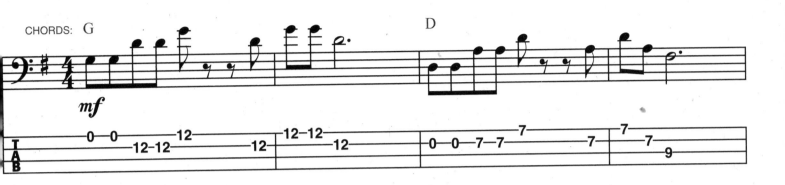

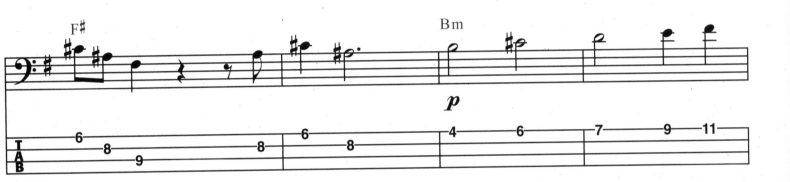

HAMMER-ONS AND PULL-OFFS

Playing smoothly from note to note is called playing *legato*. When you play legato, the notes are connected, which makes for a flowing bass line. To play more legato when playing an ascending line, you will use *hammer-ons*. When playing legato in a descending line, you will use *pull-offs*.

Playing Hammer-ons

To play a hammer-on, start with a fingered note, such as E on the D string. Pick that string with your right hand, and without picking the string again, hammer down the 2nd finger of the left hand to play the note F.

No. 1

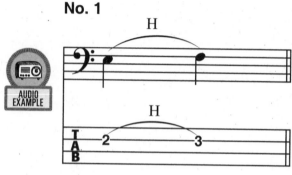

This example shows how a hammer-on is notated. The curved line, which looks a bit like a tie, is called a *slur* and connects two different notes to sound legato. The "H" stands for "hammer-on" and is not used in all sheet music. The key to knowing when to play a hammer-on is to look for the slur on ascending notes.

No. 2

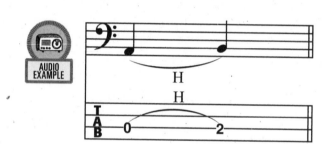

When playing a hammer-on from an open string, pick the open string, and then hammer on with the left-hand finger without picking the string again. In the next example, pick the open A string and then hammer on with the 2nd finger on the 2nd fret.

Playing Pull-offs

To play a pull-off, start with a fingered note, such as B on the G string, 4th fret. Pick that string with the 1st finger on A and the 3rd finger on B. Pull the 3rd finger off the string with a downward motion so that the A sounds clearly. As the 3rd finger pulls off the string, it is actually plucking that string to sound the A.

No. 1

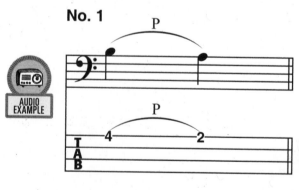

This example shows how a pull-off is notated. The slur connects the notes to sound legato. The "P" stands for "pull-off" and is not used in all sheet music. The key to knowing when to play a pull-off is to look for the slur on descending notes.

No. 2

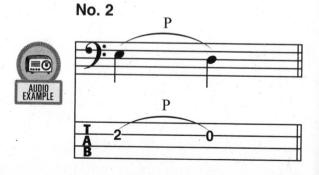

When playing a pull-off to an open string, pick a fingered note and then pull off with the left hand without picking the string again, letting the open string ring. In the next example, finger the note E on the 2nd fret of the D string with the 2nd finger. Then pull off with the 2nd finger letting the note D ring.

PLAYING THE BLUES FROM LEAD SHEETS

The 12-bar blues progression is rooted in African-American work songs from the 19th century. The blues has been used in countless songs from the earliest printed blues (St. Louis Blues in 1914) and 1950s rock songs like "Hound Dog" and "Johnny B. Goode," to songs by Led Zeppelin and artists charting today.

The blues is almost always played in major keys and follows the following basic chord pattern in which each Roman numeral stands for one measure:

| I | I (or IV7) | I | I7 | IV(7) | IV(7) | I | I | V7 | IV7 | I | I (or V7 to repeat) |

The following examples show you blues progressions in all the most commonly used keys.

Blues in E

CHORDS: E   E or A⁷ E   E⁷ A⁽⁷⁾ A⁽⁷⁾ E   E   B⁷ A⁷ E   E or B⁷

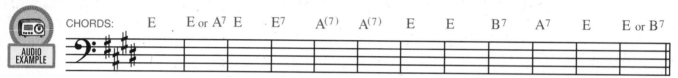

Blues in A

CHORDS: A   A or D⁷ A   A⁷ D⁽⁷⁾ D⁽⁷⁾ A   A   E⁷ D⁷ A   A or E⁷

Blues in D

CHORDS: D   D or G⁷ D   D⁷ G⁽⁷⁾ G⁽⁷⁾ D   D   A⁷ G⁷ D   D or A⁷

Blues in G

CHORDS: G   G or C⁷ G   G⁷ C⁽⁷⁾ C⁽⁷⁾ G   G   D⁷ C⁷ G   G or D⁷

Blues in C

CHORDS: C   C or F⁷ C   C⁷ F⁽⁷⁾ F⁽⁷⁾ C   C   G⁷ F⁷ C   C or G⁷

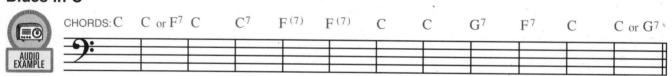

Blues in F

CHORDS: F   F or B♭⁷ F   F⁷ B♭⁽⁷⁾ B♭⁽⁷⁾ F   F   C⁷ B♭⁷ F   F or C⁷

Blues in B♭

CHORDS: B♭   B♭ or E♭⁷ B♭   B♭⁷ E♭⁽⁷⁾ E♭⁽⁷⁾ B♭   B♭⁷ F⁷ E♭⁷ B♭   B♭ or F⁷

Blues in B♭

This is a sample bass line of a B♭ blues and should be played with a swing feel. This is just one example of the blues, and you should work out bass lines in every key shown above. The best way to learn new blues bass lines is to listen to recordings of great blues players and try to play what they are playing.

Moderately fast

PART 3: STYLES

In this section, we are going to explore six essential styles you need to know as a bass player (Rock, Jazz, Funk, Reggae and Ska). You'll learn to "lock" with drums and also learn licks in the styles of legendary bassists. Let's get started with Rock.

ROCK

Rock music has gone through so many changes in its brief history that it's almost impossible to define. Artists ranging from Chuck Berry to Metallica are considered rock musicians. Get a bunch of musicians together and ask them to define rock music and they will probably all answer differently. One word you'll probably hear repeated in all the definitions however, is "attitude." Rock was built on attitude. You have to remember this when you are playing rock music. Some rock bass lines use only steady eighth notes with just the root and 5th of the chord. The conviction (attitude) of the bassist is what gives the line its character and validity, not the amount of notes. We will focus on three areas of rock bass lines: early, melodic and steady-eighth-notes and riffs style.

Early Styles

It is generally accepted that rock music began in the 1950s. Early rock bassists came from many different styles including blues, R&B, jazz, gospel and country. These styles heavily influenced early rock bass lines. The invention and widespread use of the electric bass also greatly influenced early rock styles. Like most music that originates from the United States, rock is a hybrid, or mixture, of many different styles. That is why it continues to evolve.

Melodic

Melodic bass playing became very popular in the 1960s and continues today. Because of advancements in recording technology and the volume of the electric bass, the bass line could finally be heard. In this style, the bass line has a much more interactive role and often the song revolves around the bass line. Early melodic bass innovators include Paul McCartney (Beatles), Jack Cassidy (Jefferson Airplane), Lee Sklar (James Taylor) and session players Joe Osborn (Carpenters, Mamas and the Papas) and Carole Kaye (Beach Boys).

Steady-Eighth-Notes and Riffs

Many rock bass lines are built using steady, root-based eighth notes and riffs. These are the foundation of many hard rock tunes from the 1970s to the present. Bassists that play in this style include Michael Anthony (Van Halen), Steve Harris (Iron Maiden), Tom Hamilton (Aerosmith) and Dusty Hill (ZZ Top).

Early Rock Styles

Many early rock tunes were based on the blues progression. Bassists on these early recordings used the tried and true 1, 3, 5, 6, ♭7 shuffle and walking bass patterns.

A lot of these early tunes were not much different than the popular shuffles or boogie-woogie tunes of the 1930s and '40s. In fact, this music wasn't even labeled rock'n'roll until the mid-'50s.

Rock started to get its own identity when:

1. It got away from the blues progression and started using different chord progressions.

2. Swing eighths were replaced by straight eighths.

3. Drummers started getting more inventive with their patterns.

All of these changes in the music obviously had an affect on the bass lines. Here are changes that began to appear in the bass:

1. Syncopated lines. Syncopation is a rhythmic device that shifts accents or emphasis on to the weak beats or weak parts of the beat (p. 46).

2. The use of slides, muted notes, detached notes. These are all different examples of articulation.

3. Higher pitched notes used more often.

These changes didn't happen overnight, but came about through the ideas and creativity of many bassists and composers. Below are some of the most common lines from the early rock era. Listen to how different they sound from the blues lines you already know.

DID YOU KNOW?

×= Mute. Touch the note lightly with the left hand while plucking with the right to create a percussive effect.

= Grace note. A grace note is played very quickly before the beat.

Two-Bar Patterns

One-bar Patterns

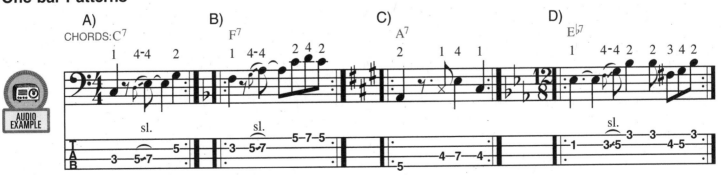

More About The I–VI–IV–V Chord Progression

One of the most frequently used chord progressions used during the early rock era, other than the blues, was the I, VI, IV, V progression (p. 90). Some tunes that use this progression are *Teenager In Love* by Dion and The Belmonts, *Sh-Boom* by the Chords and *Every Breath You Take*, a huge hit for The Police in the mid-1980s. Here's what the progression looks like in standard chord notation:

Notice that all the chords are major except for the vi chord, which is minor. If your bass line for this progression outlines the chords, make sure the vi chord has a minor quality (a ♭3). Also, keep the transitions smooth from chord to chord by using step-wise or diatonic movement. Below are some typical I, vi, IV, V progressions.

Four-Bar Patterns

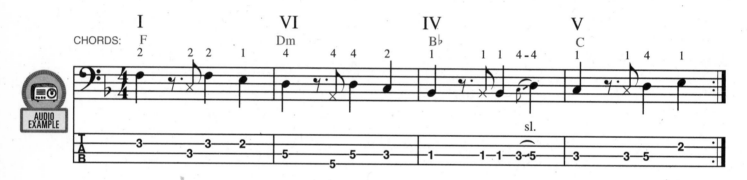

Two-Bar Patterns

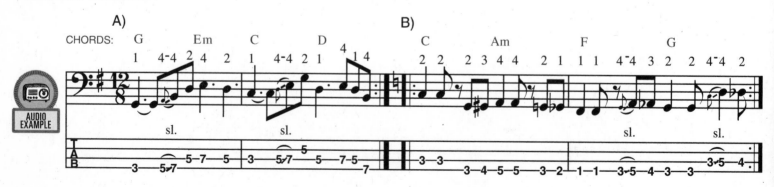

Melodic Bass

During the 1960s, rock musicians started using more complex chords, progressions and song forms. There was also a lot of experimentation going on as musicians utilized all the possibilities of the recording studio. This is when the melodic bass style began to take shape. The overall sound and abilities of bassists greatly improved during this period, which allowed the bass to play a much more prominent role in the music. Bass lines no longer centered on one- or two-bar repetitive patterns, but continually evolved throughout the song.

Before you get started building bass lines in this style, remember:

In the melodic style, the bass still functions in a supportive role!

Don't confuse melodic playing with soloing. They are two different things. Even though your bass lines are "busier" than in previous styles, they still have to GROOVE!

Here are some general characteristics and techniques of this style:

1. Varied use of rhythm—sixteenths, eighths, syncopation.
2. Varied use of diatonic and chromatic passing tones. Passing tones are tones that we pass through on our way between chord tones. Diatonic passing tones are tones that belong in the key. Chromatic passing tones are tones not found in the key.
3. Non-repetitive lines.
4. Varied use of slides and upper register playing.
5. Varied use of 3rds, 5ths and 7ths, not always root based.

These are just some basic ideas for you to examine in this style. Turn the page and start creating some melodic lines!

? DID YOU KNOW?

Paul McCartney's use of the melodic line in songs with the Beatles was revolutionary for its time. His influence on bassists can still be heard in contemporary rock.

Photo courtesy of Star File Photo, Inc.

Throughout these examples you will see this rhythm:

This is one of the most common rhythms in rock music, as well as many other styles. Get used to recognizing this pattern and use it with different articulations.

In these examples, you will also see chords written like this: **A/G   F/A   B♭/C**

These are often called slash chords. In a slash chord, the bass plays a note other than the root. What a concept! These chords are quite common in many styles so watch out for them! The top letter is the chord, and the bottom is the bass note.

The following patterns should be played with a straight-eighth-note feel.

Pattern No. 1

Pattern No. 2

On the next page, you will be introduced to the glissando and a new rhythm. A *glissando* (also called a *gliss*) is produced by attacking a note and sliding your fretting hand either up or down the neck. A gliss is written like this:

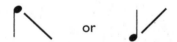

The new rhythm you will encounter on the next page should be counted like this:

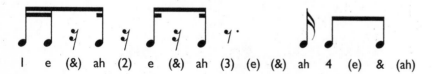

Practice this rhythm slowly, clapping and counting and then plucking open strings and counting. When you can play it accurately, and only then, increase the tempo.

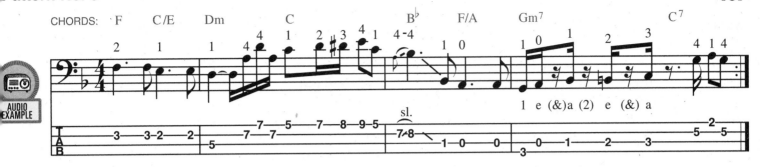

Pattern No. 4

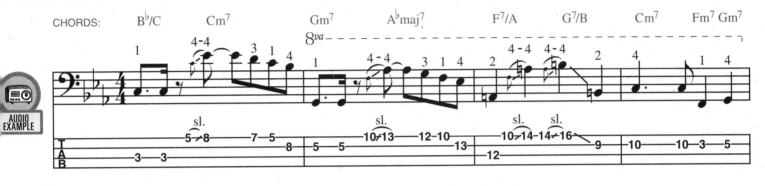

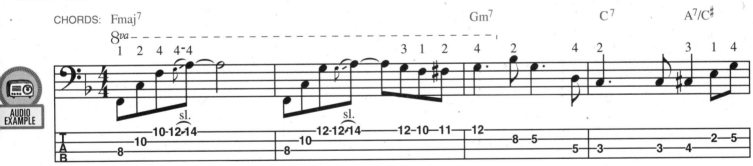

The symbol 8va (*all' ottava*) means to play the music one octave higher. The TAB is in the correct octave.

DID YOU KNOW?

Pattern No. 5

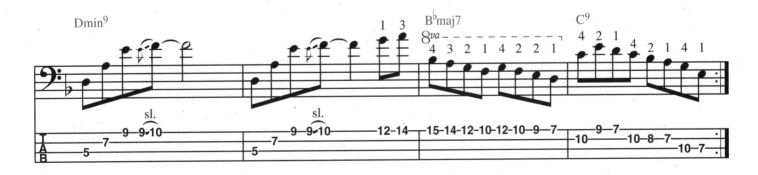

Steady-Eighth-Note & Riff Style

The bass lines we're going to check out in this section are very different from the melodic styles of the last section. This is driving, "meat and potatoes," or for you vegetarians, "tofu and potatoes," style bass. These lines are based on steady eighth notes in every measure, using primarily roots and 5ths. This kind of bass playing is usually associated with "hard-rock" or "heavy metal" music (ZZ Top, Van Halen, Aerosmith, Metallica, etc). Because the guitar is so prominent in these styles, the bass generally plays a very supportive role (with exceptions to Billy Sheehan of The David Lee Roth Band and Mr. Big). *Riffs* are also used in this style. A riff is a short, repetitive pattern that is often doubled by the guitarist. (for example, *Smoke On The Water* by Deep Purple).

PHOTO CREDIT   CHUCK PULIN / COURTESY OF STAR FILE, INC.

DID YOU KNOW?

Michael Anthony started playing bass in the 1970s with California rock group, Van Halen. They are one of the most popular rock groups in the world. He is shown here with ex-singer, Sammy Haggar and guitarist, Eddie Van Halen.

Playing consistent eighth notes with solid time and groove takes a lot of stamina and musicality. Remember, the bass line serves the tune. Even within the limitations of this style, there are lots of variations you can use with your bass lines to support and propel the music.

Here are some ideas:

1. Break up the steady eighth pattern with rests and ties.
2. Vary the eighth-note pattern with sixteenths and quarter notes.
3. Use passing tones (not too many).
4. Use octaves to break up the eighth notes.

In this style, you will often see chords written like this: "E5" or "A5," etc. These are chords that contain only the root and 5th and no 3rd; therefore, these chords do not sound either major or minor.

The following examples will utilize all the ideas mentioned above. Start rockin'!

Four-Bar Patterns

Using ties and passing tones.

Using rests.

Adding sixteenth notes.

Two-Bar Riff Patterns

Early Rock Tune

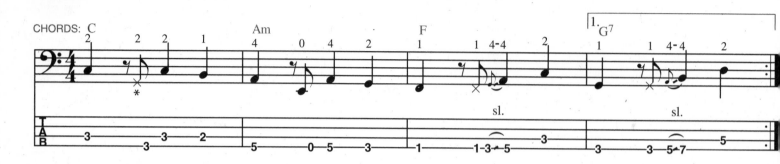

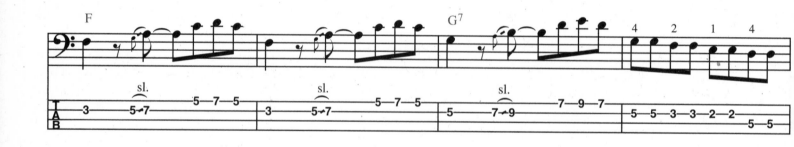

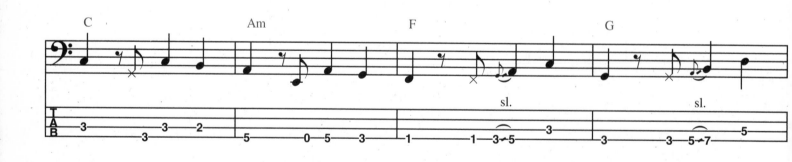

* See page 103

In this next tune, notice the Maj7 and min9 chords. They add color and richness to the harmonies. You can review chord formulas on page 73 and study basic chord theory on page 217.

Melodic Bass Tune

While this tune has mostly a steady-eighth rhythm, it starts with a funky, syncopated two-bar riff that is repeated. Learn the rhythm before trying the tune. Here's how you count it:

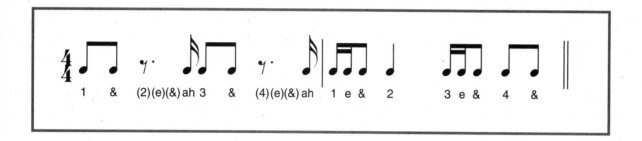

 ## Steady-Eighth-Note/Riff Tune

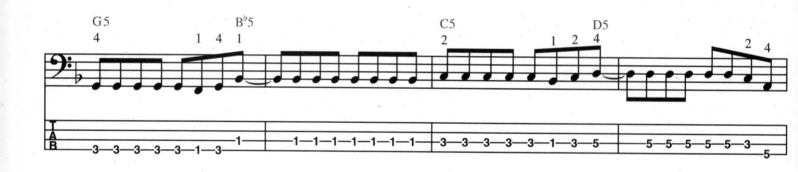

Rock Discography

Early Rock

Artist/Group	Recording	Label
Chuck Berry	*Chuck Berry The Great Twenty Eight*	Chess
Fats Domino	*Fats Domino's Greatest Hits*	MCA
Elvis Presley	*Elvis Golden Records*	RCA
Little Richard	*Little Richard's Grooviest Original Hits*	Specialty
Various Artists	*Atlantic Rhythm And Blues 1947-1974*	Atlantic
Various Artists	*Phil Spector Back To Mono*	AKO
Various Artists	*The Rock And Roll Era 1954-1965*	Time-Life Music

Bassists from this era include: Bill Black, Lloyd Trotman, Robert Parker and Wendell Marshall.

Melodic Rock

Artist/Group	Recording	Label	Bassist
The Beach Boys	*The Rock and Roll Era, The Beach Boys*	Time-Life Music	Carole Kaye
The Beatles	*Any album from Rubber Soul on*	Apple	Paul McCartney
James Taylor	*JT*	Warner Brothers	Lee Sklar
The Carpenters	*Greatest Hits*	A&M	Joe Osborn
Jefferson Airplane	*The Jefferson Airplane Loves You*	RCA	Jack Cassady
Paul Young	*Between Two Fires*	Columbia	Pino Palladino
Joni Mitchell	*Don Juan's Reckless Daughter*	Elektra	Jaco Pastorius

Eighth Note/Riff Style

Any album by the following groups:

Group	Bassist
Van Halen	Michael Anthony
Kiss	Gene Simmons
ZZ Top	Dusty Hill
Iron Maiden	Steve Harris
Aerosmith	Tom Hamilton
AC/DC	Cliff Williams

JAZZ

Jazz has had an influence on almost all musical styles of this century. The origin of the rhythm section (bass, keyboards, guitar and drums) and their specific roles comes from jazz. Walking bass and the concept of groove between the bassist and the drummer, are also jazz innovations. Jazz music has so many different styles and categories, it's almost impossible to define.

Here's a list of some general characteristics that are frequently found in jazz:

1. **Improvisation**

2. **Swing eighths**

3. **Complex harmony**

4. **More chord changes**

5. **Faster tempos**

6. **Mainly instrumental**

7. **Frequent change of key or tonal areas**

All of these characteristics have definitely had an affect on the bass line. A lot of innovations in the "bass world" have come from jazz, including walking bass and bass as a soloing instrument. As you have learned in the last two chapters, walking bass is the foundation for bass lines in many different styles. This is also true in jazz. Because this book is about building bass lines, we'll focus on jazz walking bass and save soloing for another book.

Here are some general characteristics that jazz bassists frequently use to create walking lines:

1. **Use of many non-chord tones, also called chromaticism**

2. **Rhythmic variation**

3. **Entire range of the bass used**

4. **Double stops (playing two notes at the same time)**

5. **Legato* quarter notes**

6. **Swing eighth notes**

7. **Non-repetitive, improvised**

8. **Muted notes**

In jazz, walking bass lines are often played in the legato style. In this style, notes are played smoothly and evenly. Walking bass lines in other styles (rock and blues, for example) are usually played a little more detached or separated.

Let's build some swingin' jazz walks. Dig?

Jazz Blues & Walking Bass

For our first walking bass examples, we will use the jazz blues progression. The jazz blues progression is similar to the blues progression you've already learned, but it does have some differences.

Notice the I, VI, II, V turnaround in the last two bars and the dominant 7 VI chord (VI7). These are commonly used in jazz tunes. Here's the jazz blues progression in F Major:

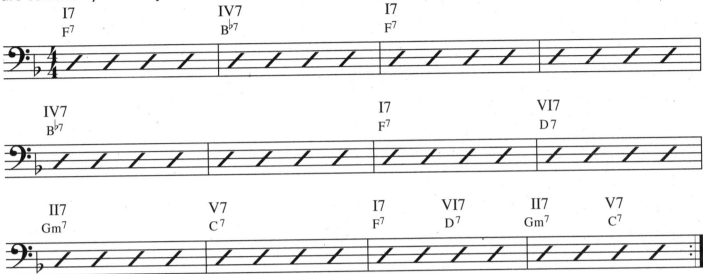

Here's a typical jazz walking bass line using many of the characteristics listed on page 114. Because of the importance of improvisation in jazz, your lines should constantly change and support the soloist. Being able to improvise a walking bass line over any set of chord changes is a required skill for jazz bassists. Notice the way scales, passing tones and arpeggios are used to create the lines. Start slowly and increase the tempo as you gain confidence.

REMEMBER: Walk before you run!

In *swing feel*, eighth notes are played unevenly. They sound like a triplet with the first two notes tied.

The II-V-I Chord Progression

The II-V-I progression can be heard in thousands of tunes played by jazz musicians. These tunes are often called *standards*. Some examples of jazz standards are *All The Things You Are*, *In A Mellow Tone* and *Autumn Leaves*. A good jazz musician will have hundreds of standards memorized and is able to play them in different keys. Memorizing chord changes may seem like an awesome task, but if you learn to see and hear the II-V-I progression, it will become easier. This is because so many jazz standards are constructed with repeated II-V-I progressions.

Here is the II-V-I progression in the key of C Major. Notice how the II and the V make you want to hear the I. It is a very logical sounding progression:

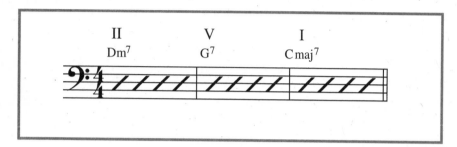

Learn this progression in every key and start checking out jazz standards that use it. A good place to start would be the example on page 117.

The examples below show the II-V-I progression in different keys with some sample walking bass lines.

No. 1

No. 2

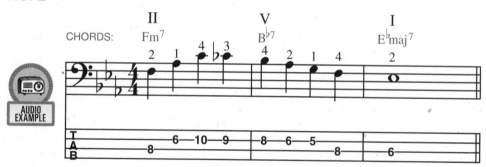

No. 3

Two-Beat & Double Stops

The two-beat feel is a common groove used by jazz bassists. This groove uses *double-stops* (two note played at once) and eighth notes in various rhythmic combinations to "break up" the four-to-the-bar walking bass pattern. This feel is often used in ballads or in the beginning of tunes before kicking into a walking bass pattern.

Below is a two-beat bass line on a jazz chord progression. Notice the frequent changes from key to key throughout this example. They are indicated to make them easy for you to find. These changes of key are accomplished with the well-known, well-used II-V-I progression. These three chords from any key have the effect of establishing the key in our ears. So, if you string a bunch of II-V-I progressions from different keys in a row, it will sound like the key is constantly changing.

Bebop & Chord Substitutions

Bebop is a style of jazz that developed during the 1940s. Bebop expanded on the harmonies and tempos of previous jazz styles (Dixieland and swing) and created a new musical "language" that is still spoken today. Charlie Parker and Dizzy Gillespie were pioneers of this style. It's important to understand the concepts of the bebop era because they are used very often in modern jazz. We'll focus on the most common bebop concept, *tritone chord substitutions*. Please read the following information SLOWLY. If you take your time and let it sink in, even complicated ideas can seem easy!

Substitution is the art of replacing an expected chord with another that accomplishes the same goal but with greater interest or surprise. *Tritone substitution* replaces one dominant 7th chord with another dominant 7th chord. The root of the substituted chord must be a tritone (an *interval* or distance of #4 or ♭5) away from the original chord. For instance, a G7 could be replaced by a D♭7 (G=1, A=2, B=3, C=4, D=5—now flat the 5, which is D, and you have a tritone). This substitution works because both chords share the most important notes—the 3 and ♭7. The interval between the 3 and ♭7 of any dominant 7th chord (a tritone, by the way) is responsible for its unique sound. In a tritone substitution, the 3 of the substituted chord is the same as the ♭7 of the original chord. The ♭7 of the substituted chord is the same as the 3 of the original chord.

Look at the example below:

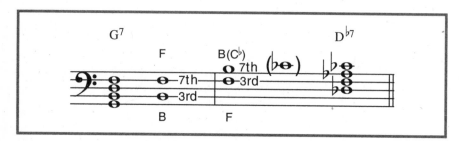

Tritone substitutions are very effective when they are applied to a II-V-I progression.

Notice the chromatic movement in the bass. This creates harmonic interest and it also sounds cool!

Here's a tritone substitution applied to a I, VI, II, V progression. The substitutions are given in parenthesis.

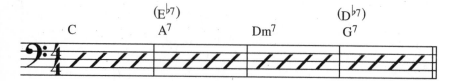

Now that you understand this harmonic device, go back and apply it to earlier examples from this chapter. Always use tritone substitutions with taste. Don't overuse them!

The following thirty-two bar form is in the style of the chord changes ("changes" is jazz lingo for "chord progression") to George Gershwin's tune, *I Got Rhythm*. These chord changes have been the basis for countless jazz tunes including *Oleo*, *Lester Leaps In* and *Shaw Nuff*. In fact, the changes are so common that jazz musicians call them *rhythm changes*. Jazzers use these changes often because there are many opportunities for chord substitutions.

In the following tune, the substitutions are in parentheses. Use the 1, 3, 5 and 7 of all the chords in your bass line and memorize this progression. Pick a slow tempo so you have time to think.

Rhythm Changes in B♭

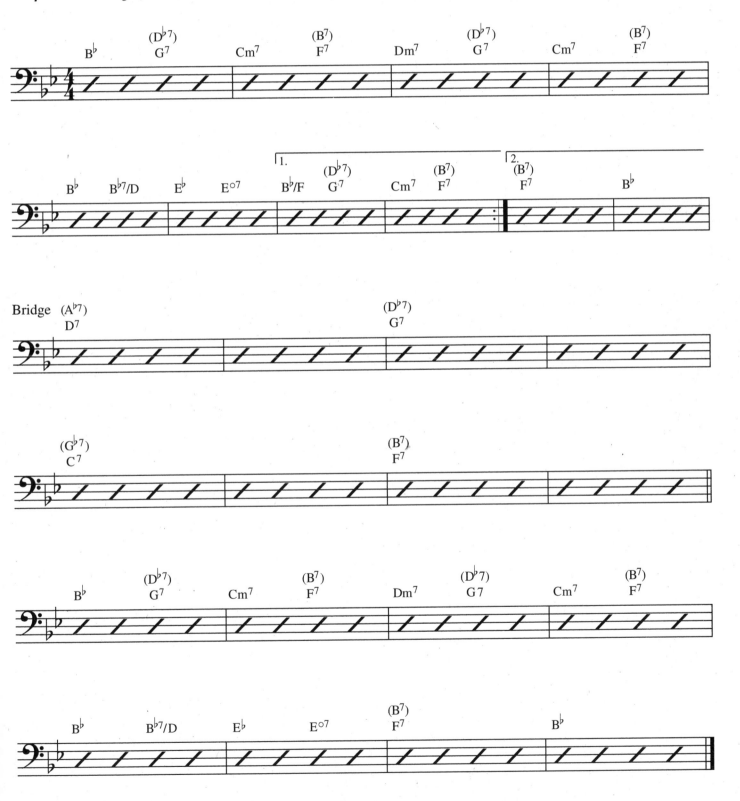

Bebop Tune on Rhythm Changes

Play twice

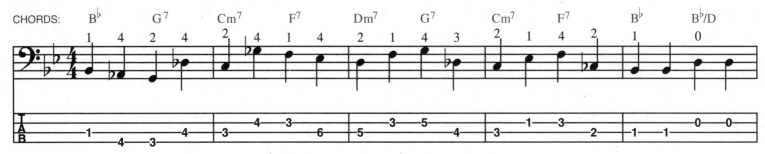

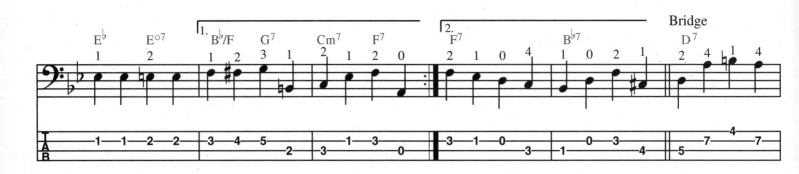

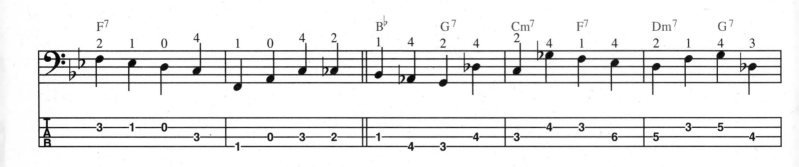

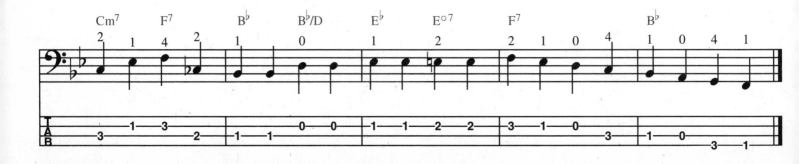

Tritone Substitutions Variation

The substitutions are in parentheses.

Swing originated around 1930, around the time New Orleans style jazz was declining in popularity. It has always defied definition, but it is characterized by a greater emphasis on solo improvisation, bigger bands and a more equal weight given to each beat of the bar (the style is sometimes called "four-beat jazz). Notice the use of the two-beat feel (page 117) in the first eight bars.

Jazz Swing Tune

Jazz Summary and Discography (Walking Bass)

Walking bass, or "four-beats-to-the-bar" is the most commonly used bass pattern in jazz. A good walking bass line should provide rhythmic, harmonic and even melodic support to the music. Because of the importance of improvisation in jazz, walking bass lines should also sound spontaneous and be interactive with the soloist. Walking bass is the foundation of most jazz tunes, so having thorough knowledge of this style is a must for bassists playing jazz. Here's a list of recordings containing some great walking bass lines. Start listening and then start walking!

Artist/Group	Recording	Label	Bassist
Cannonball Adderley	Somethin' Else	Blue Note	Sam Jones
John Coltrane	Blue Trane	Blue Note	Paul Chambers
Miles Davis	Cookin'	Prestige	Paul Chambers
Miles Davis	The Complete Concert	Columbia	Ron Carter
Bill Evans	Sunday At The Village Vanguard	Riverside	Scott La Faro
Errol Garner	Concert By the Sea	Columbia	Eddie Calhoun
Hank Jones	Love For Sale	Inner	Buster Williams
Modern Jazz Quartet	European Concert	Atlantic	Percy Heath
Charlie Parker	Jazz At Massey Hall	Prestige	Charles Mingus
Oscar Peterson	The Trio	Verve	Ray Brown
Horace Silver	Horace Silver Trio	Blue Note	Percy Heath
Teddy Wilson	Mr. Wilson and Mr. Gershwin	Columbia	Arvell Shaw

FUNK

Funk (fungk), n, a style of music that requires a bassist to simultaneously play loose yet tight on both complex rhythms with simple harmonies, or simple rhythms with complex harmonies, while still retaining a GROOVE that makes everybody move.

Now *that's* a definition!

From the simple grooves of Booker T. and the M.G.'s, to the intricate grooves of Earth, Wind and Fire, to the thrash/punk grooves of the Red Hot Chili Peppers, funk music definitely has some wide boundaries. Within these various funk grooves, however, one thing remains constant:

THE BASS LINE RULES!

That's a fact. There is no other style of music where the bass line has such a prominent role. A solid bass line is crucial in this music because funk is built from the bottom up. Although some funk bass lines can be very complex, they still have to groove and support the music. Keep that in mind when you are building funk bass lines.

Sooner or later "the FUNK is gonna getcha," so here's a list of some common characteristics of this style:

> 1. **Repetitive patterns**
> 2. **Locking-in**
> 3. **Continuous line**
> 4. **Thumb/slap/popping**

These techniques will be covered extensively in this chapter so get ready to get funky!

PHOTO © Lissa Wales

? DID YOU KNOW?

Flea, bass player of the Red Hot Chili Peppers, introduced funky, thumb-slapping techniques to a generation of alternative rockers.

Funk Bass Techniques

Funk bassists have developed techniques that have revolutionized the instrument. Below is a key that shows you how these techniques will be notated. If you are an arranger and writing out lines for a player, try using the symbols shown for these techniques. Please read this section thoroughly!

Using these techniques in various combinations can produce limitless funk bass lines. Please note that the instructions describing the techniques are written for right-handed players. Lefties can reverse them.

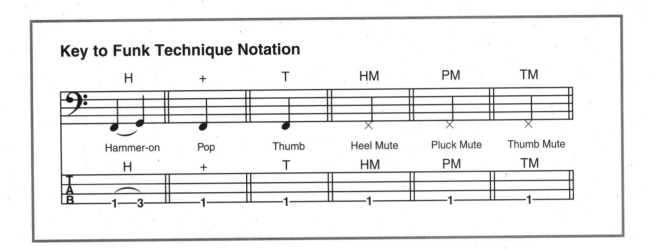

Key to Funk Technique Notation

Technical Instructions

H = hammer on: Strike the string with your right hand. While the string is ringing, re-attack with your left hand to create a new note.

+ = pop: Pull the string out with any right-hand finger causing it to bounce against the frets making a percussive sound.

T = thumb slap: Strike the string with the thumb of your right hand.

HM = heel mute: Strike the string with the heel of your right hand while muting the same string with your left hand.

PM = pluck mute: Pluck the string with your right hand while muting the same string with your left hand.

TM = thumb mute: Strike the string with your right hand thumb while muting the same string with your left hand.

Repetitive Style

As you have seen and heard in previous chapters, many bass lines are built using repetitive one or two bar patterns. Funk bass lines also use this technique and are often the "hook" or most recognizable part of the tune. Some classic repetitive bass lines can be heard on the tunes such as *It's The Same Old Song* by The Four Tops (played by James Jamerson), *Funky Broadway* by Wilson Pickett (played by Tommy Cogbill) and *Papa's Got A Brand New Bag* by James Brown (played by Sam Thomas). Below are some funk bass patterns ranging from simple to complex.

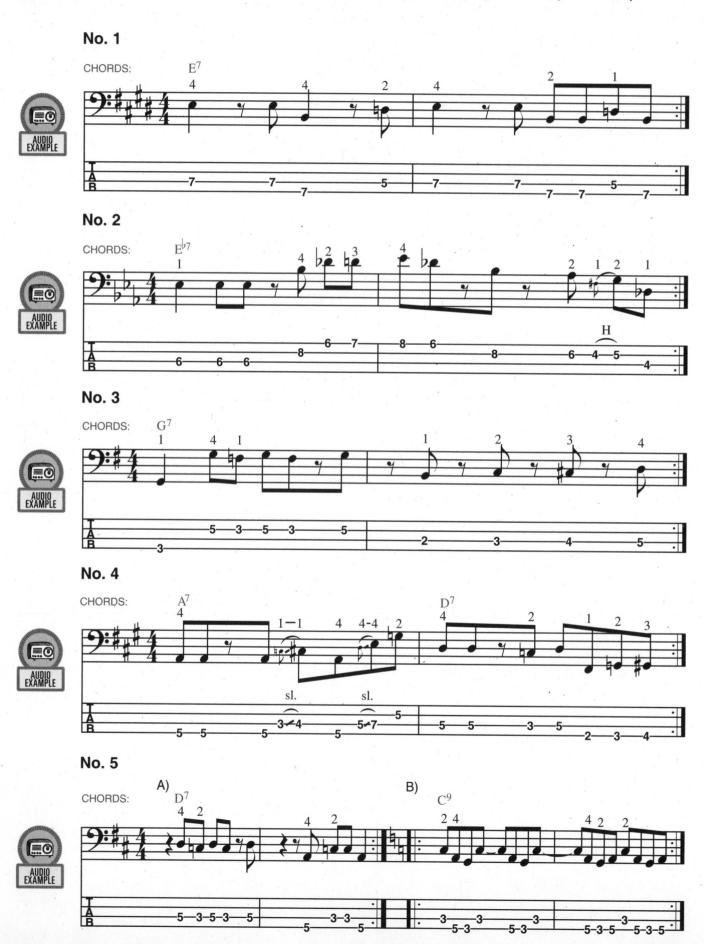

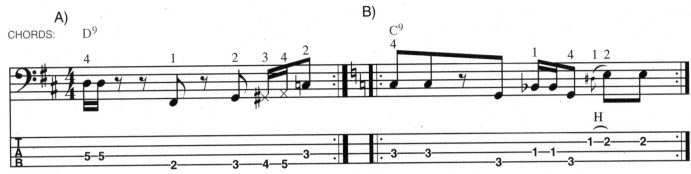

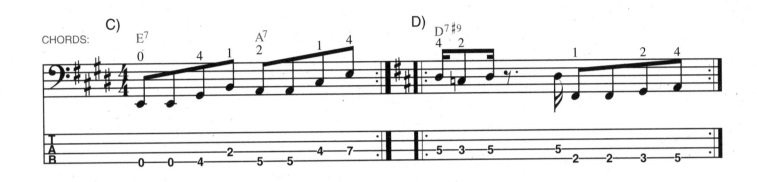

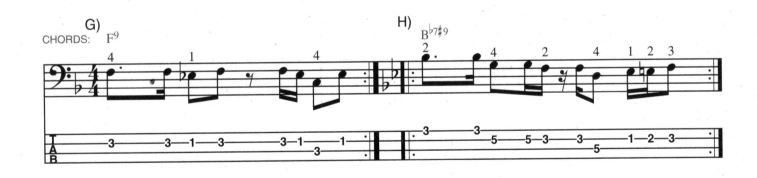

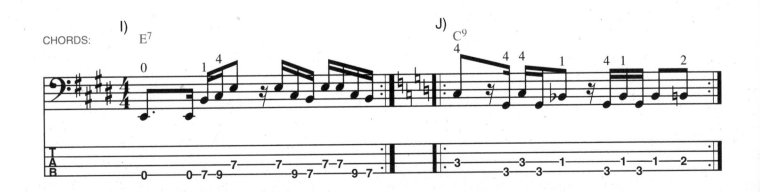

Continuous Line

A *continuous line* is created using continuous sixteenth or eighth notes (depending on the tempo) broken up by syncopated mutes, rests and passing tones. This style is very "busy," both rhythmically and harmonically. It is also highly improvisational. This type of line should only be used in the correct context, where the rest of the instruments are playing very sparsely, and the bass is almost soloing. Some examples of this style are *What Is Hip?* by Tower Of Power (played by Rocco Prestia), *Come On Come Over* by Jaco Pastorius (played by Jaco Pastorius) and *Benadette* by The Four Tops (played by James Jamerson). Here are some continuous-line examples. Practice these lines slowly and make sure you are playing each note evenly with good time. Then work them up to the suggested tempos. Let's be careful out there!

No. 1

No. 2

No. 3

No. 4

Jaco Pastorius was a brilliant bassist who was adept in jazz and funk styles. In the 1970s he played with the fusion group, Weather Report, which also featured saxophonist, Wayne Shorter and pianist, Joe Zawinul. In the early '80s he toured with his big band, Word of Mouth. Tragically, he died in 1987 at the age of 35.

PHOTO CREDIT   DAVID SEELIG / COURTESY OF STAR FILE INC.

No. 5

CHORDS: C⁹   B♭⁹

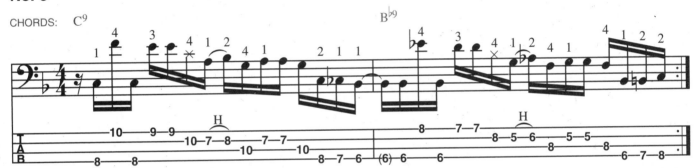

No. 6

CHORDS: Gm⁹

No. 7

CHORDS: G⁹   C⁹

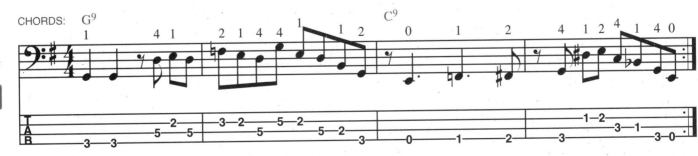

No. 8

No. 9

No. 10

Thumb Slap & Pop and Locking-In Techniques

The *thumb slap & pop* technique has become synonymous with funk bass playing. Pioneered by Larry Graham (bassist for Sly and the Family Stone and leader of Graham Central Station), this technique uses the thumb and all four fingers of the right hand. Striking down on the strings with the thumb (slapping) and plucking (popping) with any finger (usually the index or middle), produces a very percussive effect. Adding mutes, slides and hammer-ons gives the bassist even more rhythmic variation. As with all techniques, don't overuse it in your playing or arrangements or it will become stale very fast. Some examples of this style are *Pow* by Graham Central Station (played by Larry Graham), *Run For Cover* by David Sanborn (played by Marcus Miller) and *Me And My Bass Guitar* by Victor Wooten (played by Victor Wooten).

Locking-in is another funk concept that is often used in conjunction with the slap & pop technique. Locking-in occurs when the bass line is in rhythmic unison (exactly together) with the rhythmic pattern of the bass drum. This is very effective and creates a serious groove! Bass and drums should work together in all styles, so you bass players should practice with a "real" drummer (not just a drum machine) whenever possible. Some examples of great locking-in can be found in *Shining Star* by Earth, Wind And Fire (played by Verdine White) and *She's A Super Lady* by Luther Vandross (played by Marcus Miller). Here's a whole bunch of funky lines so "lock-in" and "throwdown!"

No. 1

No. 2

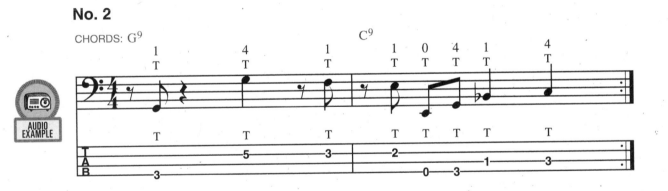

No. 3

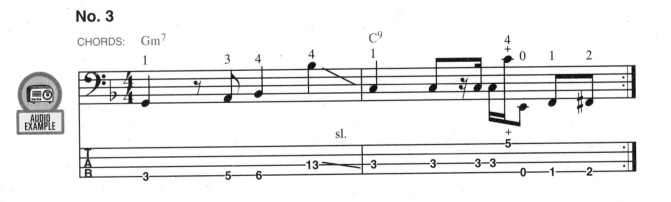

132

No. 4

CHORDS: B♭m7   E♭9

No. 5

CHORDS: D7♯9

No. 6

CHORDS: Gm7

No. 7

CHORDS: E7♯9

No. 8

CHORDS: Am7   D7

Last Call For Thumbs

Just to give your thumb technique a bit more of a workout, here are some patterns using the open E string. Try playing these patterns in other keys. Not all funk tunes are in the key of E, although it sometimes seems like they are!

No. 1

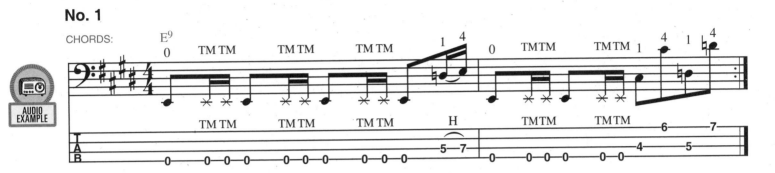

No. 2

No. 3

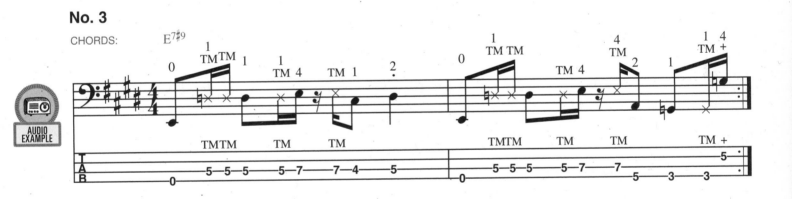

No. 4

Continuous-Line Funk Tune

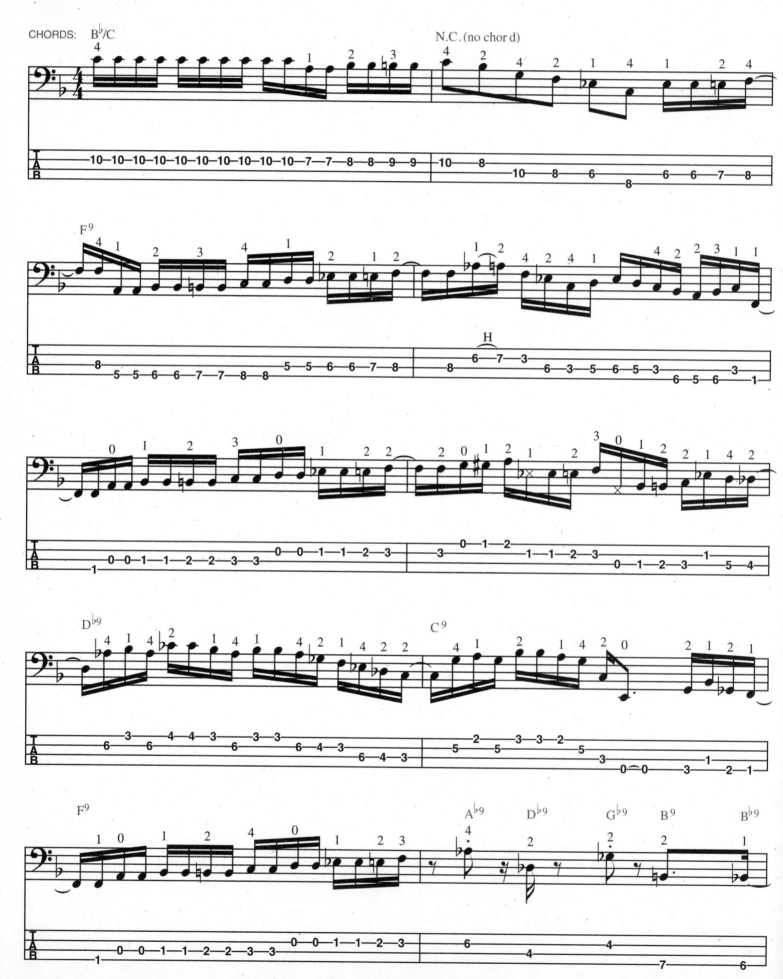

Thumb Funk

Repetitive-Line Funk

Funk Summary & Discography

The bass is the most prominent instrument in funk music. A funky bass line is the backbone
to countless funk tunes and is the most essential element in this style. A funk bass line can be
very simple or extremely complex, but it should be "in the pocket" and grooving at all times. In
the words of Bootsy Collins "One nation under a groove y'all." Here are some recordings and
bassists that should give you some funky inspiration:

Artist/Group	Recording	Label	Bassist
Brecker Brothers	The Brecker Brothers	Atlantic	Will Lee
James Brown	J.B. on C.D. Vols. 1 & 2	Polydo	Bernard Odum, Tim Drummond, Various
Tim Cameo	Machismo	Polygram	Various
Ray Charles	Greatest Hits	Atlantic	Various
Earth, Wind and Fire	Gratitude	Columbia	Verdine White
Marvin Gaye	Anthology	Motown	James Jamerson
Herbie Hancock	Headhunters	Columbia	Paul Jackson
Brothers Johnson	Greatest Hits	A & M	Louis Johnson
Level 42	Level 42	Polydor	Mark King
Parliament	Greatest Hits	Polygram	Bootsy Collins, Various
Jaco Pastorius	Jaco Pastorius	Epic	Jaco Pastorius
Various	Atlantic Records Anthology	Atlantic	Duck Dunn, Various
Various	The History of Funk	Rhino	Various
Red Hot Chili Peppers	Freakey Styley	EMI	Flea
Sly & the Family Stone	Greatest Hits	Epic	Larry Graham
Stevie Wonder	Musicaqaurium	Motown	Nathan Watts, Various
The Meters	Anthology	Rhino	George Porter
Tower of Power	Tower of Power	Warner	Rocco Prestia

REGGAE

Reggae music's origins can be traced to the island of Jamaica during the late 1960s. It is a mix of Caribbean folk songs, American R&B and African *polyrhythms* (two or more different rhythms being played simultaneously), blended together to create a unique style of music. Reggae is now an international style and its hypnotic rhythm is used in virtually all styles of music. Artists as diverse as Bonnie Raitt and Stevie Wonder have done the "reggae." The worldwide popularity of reggae is good news for bassists because of its important role in the music. A deep, resonant bass line is the "heartbeat" of reggae music.

Reggae bass lines are very prominent and many tunes are built around them. The bass patterns are very melodic and often rhythmically complex. In this style, bass lines, and often bass drum patterns, sometimes avoid the first beat of each measure. This pattern is called the "one drop."

A Note to Bassists

With all this syncopation, playing reggae for the first time can be a little confusing. But don't worry *mon*, you can do it! All you need to do is focus on the guitar part in reggae. The guitar is the time keeper in reggae. Most reggae guitar parts are built on the offbeats of every measure. Here's what a typical reggae guitar rhythm looks like:

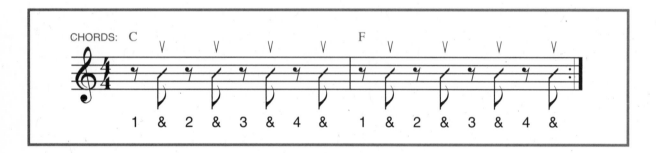

V = Upstroke

If you focus on the guitar part, you'll always know where the beat is. Also, listening to reggae is the best way to help you understand the nuances of this style.

Here's a list of general reggae bass characteristics:

1. **Repetitive, melodic patterns. Pick a groove and stay on it!**
2. **Patterns are built around triads and stepwise motion.**
3. **Lay back! Reggae bass lines should not sound rushed.**
4. **Use syncopation and rhythmic variation.**
5. **Use muted notes for variation.**
6. **Slower tempos, ♩ = 72–92 are prominent. Although written in common time, it is often best to think of reggae as having two slow beats per measure.**
7. **Playing off the downbeat is important. Always know where beat one is, but don't play on it!**

Now, start laying down some roots *riddum* and stir it up!

Below are some typical reggae bass lines. Make sure you play the rhythms accurately. The bass line is CRUCIAL in reggae music. Have fun and groove!

No. 1

No. 6

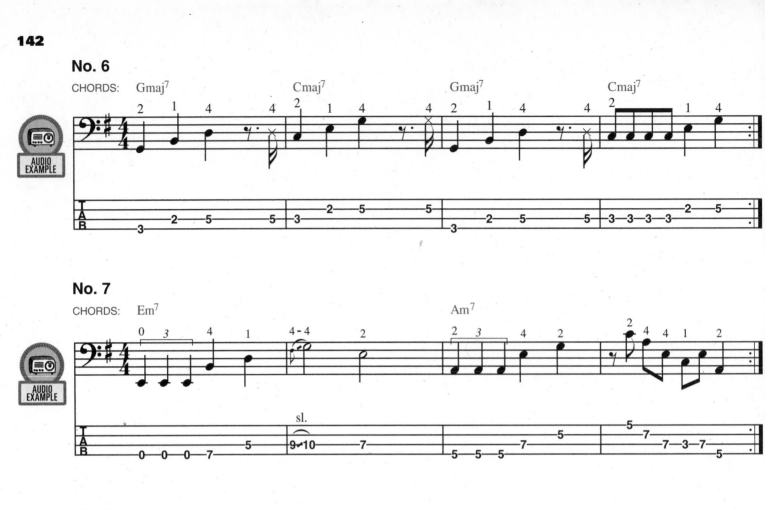

No. 7

No. 8

No. 9

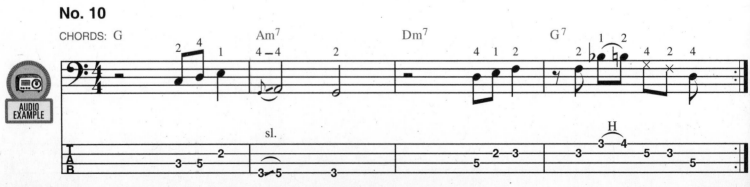

No. 10

No. 11

CHORDS: Gmaj7   Cmaj7

No. 12

CHORDS: Cm7   B♭

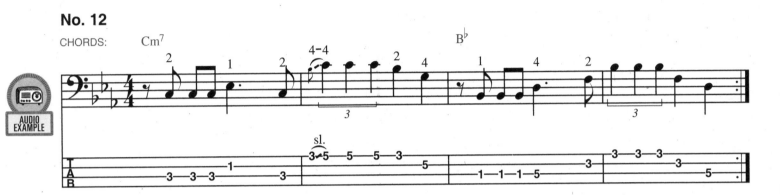

No. 13

CHORDS: Dm

No. 14

CHORDS: Am7

Dm7

Reggae Tune

Reggae Summary & Discography

Reggae bass lines are very prominent and are considered to be the "heartbeat" of reggae music. Reggae bass lines can be very syncopated and often avoid the first beat of each measure. A good reggae bass line should always sound relaxed and maintain a constant pulse. Here are some reggae recordings that should help you get in an island mood. Reggae on!

Artist/Group	Recording	Label
Black Uhuru	Red	Island/Mango
Jimmy Cliff	The Harder They Come	Mango
Gregory Isaacs	Night Nurse	Island/Mango
Toots and the Maytals	The Best of Toots	Trojan
Bob Marley and the Wailers	Legend	Island
Lee "Scratch" Perry	Reggae Greats	Mango
Shabba Ranks	As Raw As Ever	CBS
Sly and Robbie	Reggae Greats	Mango
Steel Pulse	Earth Crisis	Elektra
The Itals	Give Me Power	Nighthawk
Third World	Reggae Greats	Island
Various Artists	The King Kong Compilation	Mango
Various	This is Reggae Vols. 1-5	Mango
Various	Reggae Hits Vols. 1-16	Jetstar
Yellowman	King Yellowman	Columbia

Bassists you should check out:

Aston "Family Man" Barrett

Robbie Shakespeare

Val Douglas

Bertram McLean

Lloyd Parks

Errol (Flabba) Holt

SKA

Ska music originated in Jamaica in the early 1960s and is the predecessor to reggae. Ska was originally conceived as Jamaican styles combined with jazz and R&B from the United States. Throughout the 1970s, '80s and '90s however, ska music has been combined with many styles including rock, punk, new wave and thrash. These contemporary versions have contributed to the evolution and popularity of this unique style.

Ska music should be thought of as having (so far) two periods, early and contemporary. The early ska period encompasses the 1960s to the mid-1970s. The contemporary ska period ranges from the 1980s to the present.

Early ska was primarily an instrumental style and was pioneered by a group called The Skatalites. The Skatalites used a typical rhythm section (piano, guitar, bass and drums) and a horn section (trumpet, trombone and saxophone). This lineup continues to be used in contemporary ska bands. Because ska music preceded reggae, you may hear some similarities. The use of the guitar upbeats and the chord progressions are similar in both styles. There are differences, however, especially in the bass lines. Early ska bassists used the acoustic bass. Naturally, this affected the sound and function of the bass in this style. Keep that in mind when you are playing early ska tunes—your slap and pop electric bass techniques would be out of place!

Early ska style bass line characteristics:

1. **Tempos range from ♩ = 116 to 140.**
2. **Patterns are often built on triads and step movement (very similar to early R&B bass lines).**
3. **Patterns tend to be repetitive and are not as rhythmically complex as reggae bass lines.**
4. **Ska bass lines are not as prominent as reggae bass lines.**
5. **Acoustic bass was prevalent.**

Contemporary ska music encompasses many styles and influences that have greatly changed the role of ska bass lines. Contemporary ska bass lines are usually played on the electric bass and are much more prominent. These bass lines can be very challenging simply because of the increased tempos.

Contemporary ska style bass line characteristics:

1. **Tempos range from ♩ =160 to 240!**
2. **Has more of a rock edge.**
3. **Patterns are not as repetitive as the early style.**
4. **Electric bass is prevalent.**
5. **Harmonies are less diatonic.**

Turn the page and get into the ska groove!

Early Ska Bass Patterns

Contemporary Ska Bass Patterns

No. 1

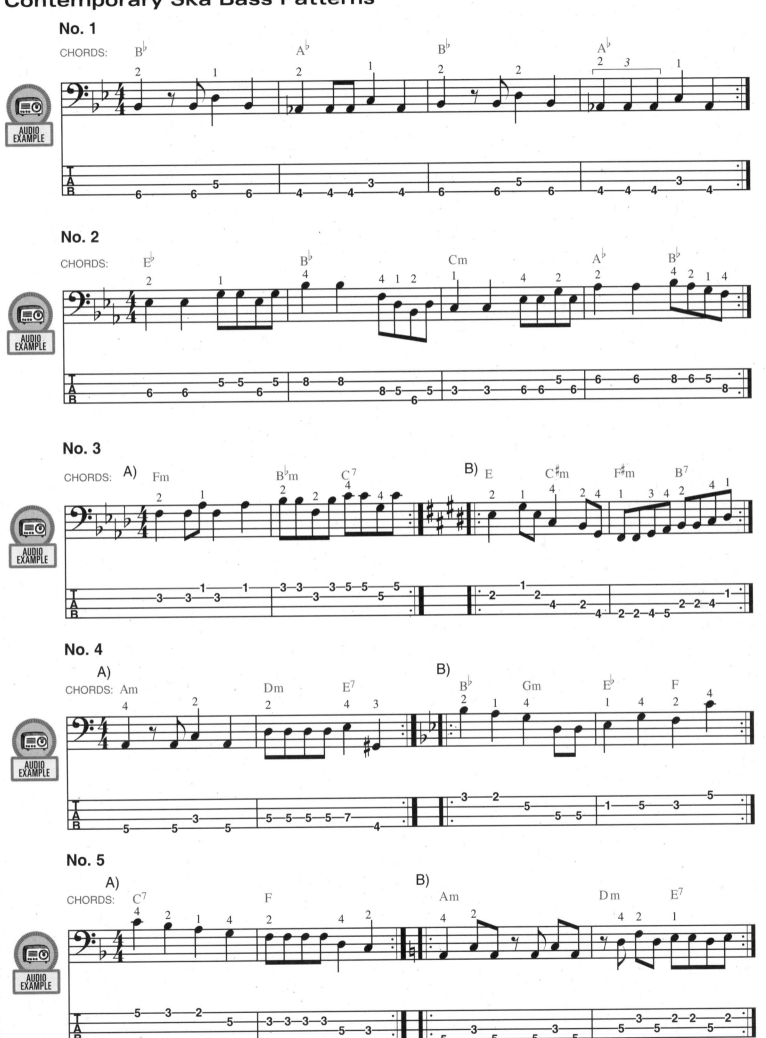

Early Ska Tune

Contemporary Ska Tune

Ska Summary & Discography

Ska is a musical style that originated in Jamaica in the early 1960s and has since become an international style. There are two styles associated with ska, early and contemporary. Early styles often used the acoustic bass and the bass lines sounded very similar to early rock bass lines from the United States. Contemporary styles combined ska with other styles including punk and funk. Contemporary ska bass lines can be very syncopated and can be difficult to play because of the fast tempos. ($\quarternote$ = 180-240!). Here are some ska recordings that should get you in a ska mood.

Keep it steady!

Early Ska

Artist/Group	Recording	Label
Ethiopians	*The World Goes Ska*	Jetstar
The Skatalites	*Foundation Ska*	Heartbeat
Various	*The Best of Studio One Vols.1 & 2*	Heartbeat
Various	*Ska Bonanza*	Heartbeat
Various	*Original Club Ska*	Heartbeat

Contemporary Ska

Artist/Group	Recording	Label
Hepcat	*Right On Time*	Hellcat Records
Less Than Jake	*Losing Streak*	Capitol
Madness	*One Step Beyond*	Two-Tone
Mighty, Mighty Bosstones	*Let's Face It*	Mercury
Skinnerbox	*What You Can Do, What You Can't*	Moon Ska Records
Slackers	*Redlight*	Hellcat Records
The Specials	*The Specials*	Chrysalis
The Pietasters	*Oolooloo*	Moon Ska Records
Toasters	*Skaboom*	Moon Ska Records

SOCA

Soca music comes from the island of Trinidad and is a mixture of two distinct styles: calypso and soul/funk music. Calypso originated in Trinidad in the nineteenth century and is considered to be the country's folk music. It is partying, carnival music that is often associated with Trinidad's steel drum bands. Soca began in the 1970s when calypso was combined with American soul and funk music. Soca is an abbreviation for "soul-calypso" and its upbeat dance groove has brought it worldwide attention. One of the most popular soca tunes is *Hot, Hot, Hot* originally recorded by Arrow and later covered by American singer Buster Poindexter. If you've heard either recording, you know that soca is very groove-oriented music and the bass line plays a big part in creating that groove!

Soca bass lines are very prominent and have a strong rhythmic and melodic feel. In fact, most soca tunes are built around the bass line. Because of the American funk/soul influence, many soca bass lines may sound familiar to those of you that have already checked out the funk section of this book. Soca is dance music that often uses a drum machine, so you bassists out there must make sure your bass lines are precise and rhythmically accurate.

Here are some general characteristics of soca style bass lines:

1. **Repetitive, melodic patterns built on triads and chromatic passing notes.**
2. **Patterns highly syncopated, often using 8th and 16th notes.**
3. **Tempos can range from ♩ = 110 - 150.**
4. **A constant, forward moving momentum that never lets up!**

You are now ready to create some serious, carnival soca grooves. Hot, Hot, Hot!

*The Banshees of Blue featuring **Buster Poindexter** (second from left), had a big hit in 1987 with **Hot, Hot, Hot**, a soca tune and one of the great party anthems of all time.*

PHOTO CREDIT BOB GRUEN / COURTESY OF STAR FILE INC.

No. 1

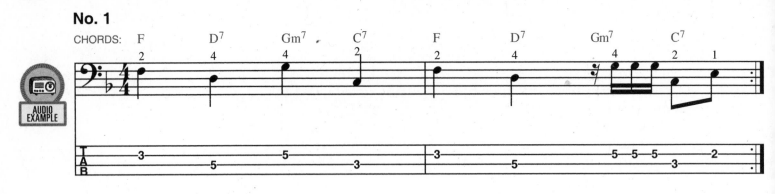

No. 2

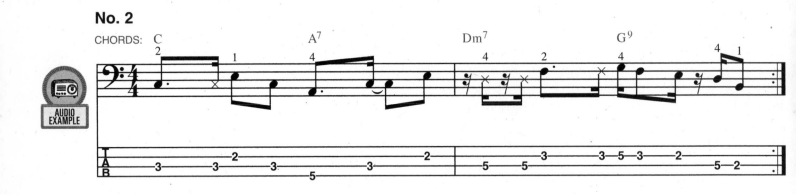

No. 3

No. 4

No. 5

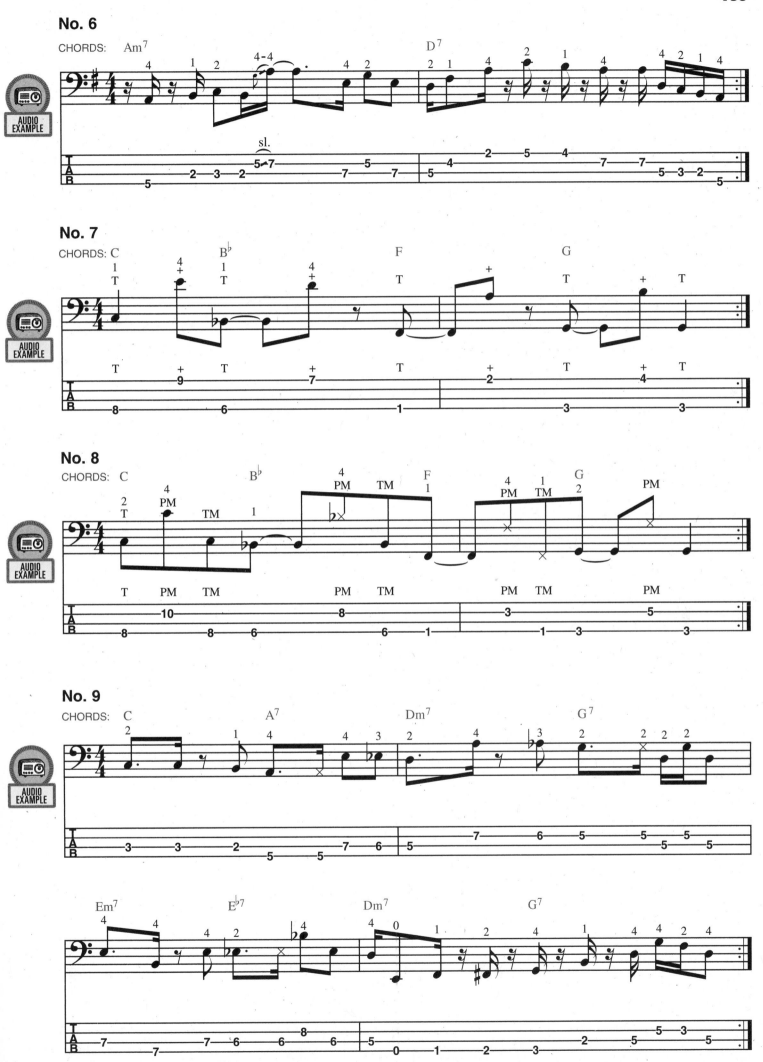

Soca Tune

Soca Summary & Discography

Soca music is a style that comes from the island of Trinidad. It is a mix of soul music from the U.S. and calypso music from Trinidad. Soca bass lines are very prominent and can be very syncopated. Because soca music is primarily dance music, bass lines should be very consistent and keep the groove moving forward. Here are some soca recordings to help you create some excellent island grooves.

Artist/Group	Recording	Label
Safi Abdullah	*Another One Gone*	Shanachie
Arrow	*O' La Soca*	Mango
Black Stalin	*Rebellion*	Ice
Burning Flames	*Dig*	Mango
Andy Narell	*The Hammer*	Hip Pocket
Nelson	*When The World Turns*	Shanachie
Singing Francine	*This is Singing Francine*	Red Bullet
The Heart of Steel	*Steelbands of Trinidad*	Flying Fish
Various	*Soca Breakdown*	Straker's
Various	*Soca Music From Trinidad*	Rounder
Various	*This is Soca*	Oval

LOCKING-IN WITH THE DRUMS

A subject that many beginning bassists tend to overlook is *grooving*, or *locking-in with the drums*. No matter how many breathtaking techniques and flashy tricks you learn, you will not be very useful to the band if you don't supply the groove. The groove is the rhythmic foundation of a tune. This has to be done precisely with the drums—by locking-in. Locking-in is the way we describe playing in exact synchronization with what the drummer is doing.

Locking-in with the drums helps the other musicians in the band sound good. The flashy techniques and tricks are simply dressing on the salad. Flea, Jaco Pastorius and Victor Wooten are all great players who can do many things, but the *first* thing they do is play killer grooves. Depending on the style of music, the bassist concentrates on locking-in with certain areas of the drum kit.

This chapter will give you two examples of bass grooves in the styles of rock, funk and reggae. The first example of each will be a bass line that *doesn't* quite lock in with the drum groove. The second example will be a bass line that *does* lock in with the drum groove. Listen and play along with the recording—you will hear the difference between these two examples. You can also have a friend play the drum part along with you as you play both examples.

Here is a key to the drum notation:

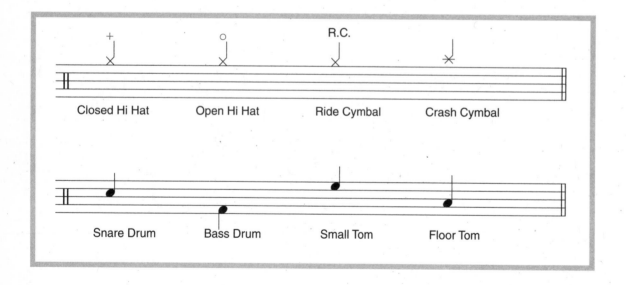

Rock Grooves

In rock music, bass players usually focus on locking-in with the bass drum. If the bass guitar does not lock-in with the bass drum in a rock tune, chances are that the groove will not be strong or driving enough; it won't make someone want to move their body.

Notice that the first bass line does not lock-in with the drum part, while the second one does—the rhythm more closely reflects that of the bass drum. It sounds much better.

This one doesn't work very well.

This one works very well.

Funk Grooves

In funk music, like rock music, the bass player usually locks-in solidly with the kick and snare drums. There is nothing more satisfying to a bass player than locking-in with the drummer in a tight funk groove. The syncopated rhythms of funk music require powerful bass and drum grooves.

Since funk is extremely "bass-oriented" music, there are two bass lines included for this style. The first example of each bass line does not work as well with the drums as the second. This is because the rhythm of the second is more closely related to that of the drums. Listen closely while you play along with a friend or the recording that comes with this book.

Funk Groove No. 1

This one doesn't work very well.

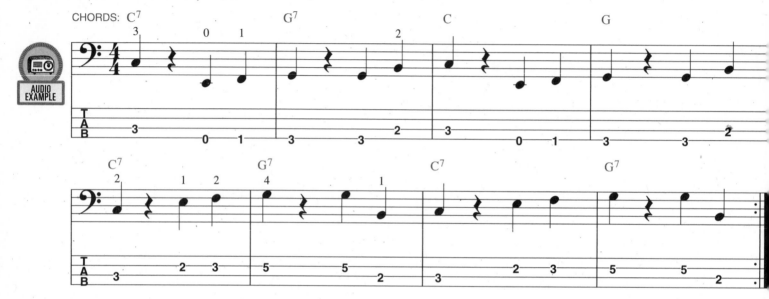

This one works very well.

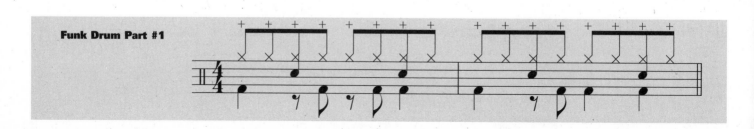

Funk Drum Part #1

Funk Groove No. 2

This one doesn't work very well.

This one works very well.

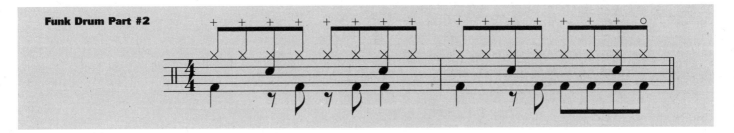

Reggae Grooves

In reggae music, the bass drum usually emphasizes the third beat of the measure. Although the bass part does not have to emphasize this beat to groove with the drums, it sounds very powerful when it does. The first bass line below does not play on the third beat and the second one does. Most people would agree that the second one sounds better, because it ties in more closely to the rhythm of the drum part.

This one doesn't emphasize the third beat.

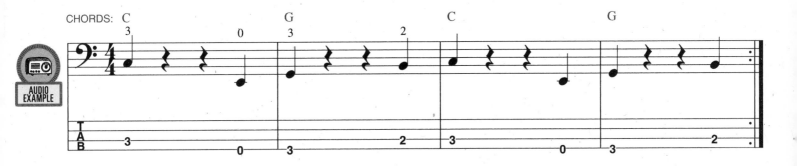

This one does emphasize the third beat. It works better than the first.

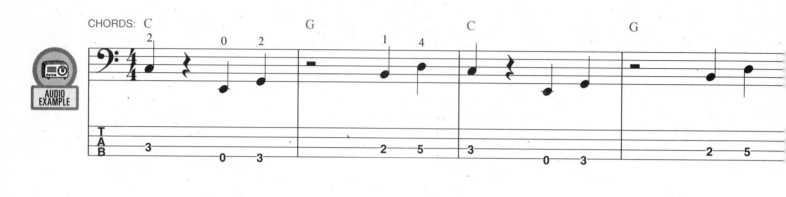

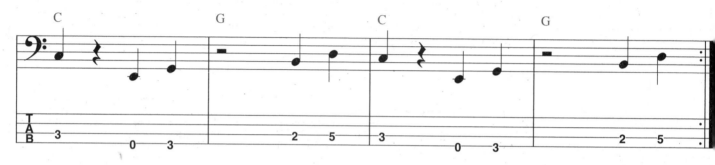

Reggae Drum Part

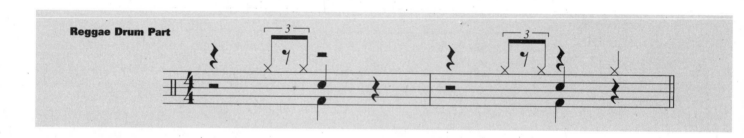

Photo courtesy of Joseph Sia/Star File Photo, Inc.

Geddy Lee
Rush is one of the most innovative supergroups of the mid-1970s. Geddy Lee's biting, complex bass lines are largly responsible for the band's unique sound.

LICKS IN THE STYLES OF FAMOUS BASS PLAYERS

 ## Geddy Lee (Rush)

 ## Randy Jackson (Billy Cobham)

Billy Sheehan

CHORDS: E5

John Pattituci

CHORDS: Emaj⁷

Slap and Pop Technique

Slapping and popping utilizes the picking hand and dictates the way the strings should be struck. Use your thumb to slap the strings with the "S" below them, and use your fingers to pop the strings with the "P" above them. To get the sound correct, you really need to slap and pop the strings with a good deal of attack.

Les Claypool (Primus)

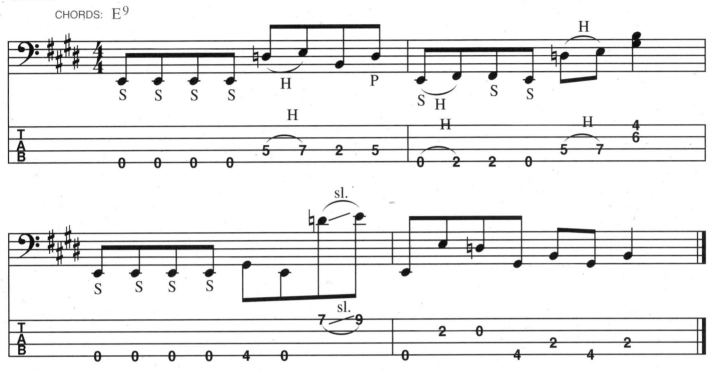

John Paul Jones (Led Zeppelin)

Michael Anthony (Van Halen)

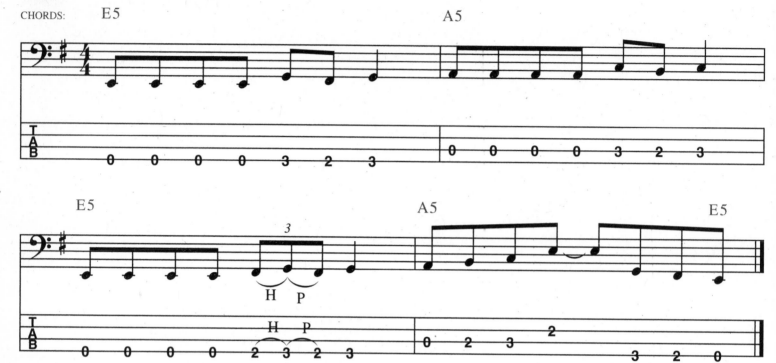

Flea (Red Hot Chili Peppers)

Roger Waters

Jaco Pastorious

168

Stanley Clarke

CHORDS: Em

Willie Dixon

CHORDS: E⁷

PART 4: BEING A PROFESSIONAL BASSIST

Playing the bass in a band is fun and rewarding. Having acquired the skills and knowledge offered in this book so far, you are probably ready to play in a band. This section of the book provides tips on starting or joining a band, preparing for an audition, rehearsing and gigging. You'll also learn how to promote yourself, and even how to practice more effectively. Finally, you'll gain some insights into the music business, discover how to protect your interests and eventually get a recording contract. Let's get started.

FINDING, REHEARSING AND PROMOTING A BAND

How to Tell If You're Ready To Play in a Band

If you can play over a dozen songs from beginning to end without many mistakes and without losing the beat, then you are ready to play in a band. For a band to play live, they need to know at least a dozen songs.

How to Start a Band

There are a number of ways to find other musicians to play with. One way is to ask an instructor if he or she has any students who might want to get together with you. Most instructors want to help their students find other people to play with, and they may already know who to suggest. This method can help you find other bassists as well as guitarists, drummers, keyboard players and any other kind of musician.

Another way to find musicians to play with is to put up an ad at your local music store. Make it brief and to the point, saying what type of players you are looking for. You can put the same ad in your local paper or classified Website. Many classified sections will charge nothing for this service.

How to Find and Get into an Existing Band

It's a good idea to talk to people that you know in the music business and ask if they know of a band that is looking for a bassist. If they're not aware of any at the time, ask if they can keep you in mind and recommend you, or at least, let you know the next time they hear of an opening. You can make a personal webpage which tells about your experience, musical preferences, and equipment. Have business cards made which include your phone number, e-mail address and webpage address. Musicians tend to help each other, and hopefully someday you'll be in a position to return the favor.

Other ways of finding bands looking for bassists are to look on bulletin boards in music stores and look in classified ads in newspapers and music magazines. You can also find bands that need bassists on the Internet. To access a number of musician referral services on the Internet, search: musician+referral service.

How to Be the One Everyone Wants in Their Band

TIPS

1. **Show up at all rehearsals on time.** When it's time to start, have your bass already tuned, your amp set and be ready to go. This shows that you are enthusiastic about playing.

2. **Have your parts learned well.** Have the song arrangements memorized. Be ready to play the songs all the way through without making a lot of mistakes. Do as much preparation as possible outside of rehearsal.

3. **Have a good attitude.** Be enthusiastic about the group and about rehearsals. A positive attitude is contagious. If you're excited about playing, the other members will pick up on it and will become enthusiastic themselves.

4. **Be a team player.** Leave your ego outside the door. Keep in mind that everyone in the group is working towards a common goal. Have respect for the other members and their opinions.

5. **Help with the business of the band.** Do all you can to help with band promotion, getting gigs and keeping track of the finances. Remember that being in a band is being part of a business.

6. **When you're not playing a song, don't play.** Just turn your volume off. This rule applies to rehearsals, sound checks and performances. Don't play at all between songs. Playing between songs can be distracting and annoying to other members of the group and to the audience.

7. **Never tune your bass aloud**. Use a silent electronic tuner, one that cuts off the signal to your amp while you tune.

8. **Learn to sing**. Finding players who can sing is a big challenge for many bands. Knowing how to sing, even a little, can be the difference between you and the other guy getting the job.

Your Personal Promotional Pack

In order to join almost any established band, you will need to try to get an audition with that band. In order to get an audition, you may need to have your own *promo pack*.

What Your Promo Pack Should Include

Your promo pack should contain:

- A photograph of yourself,
- A recording that has two or three minutes of your best playing,
- A biography that tells about your experience.

Make your promo pack as professional-looking as possible by having a good photographer take your picture, and have it enlarged into an 8x10 glossy. The recording should be one with songs that you have recorded in the studio and include parts of any songs that best demonstrate your abilities. If you can play in some different styles, be sure to include them on your recording. Versatility is always good.

If you haven't been in the studio, record yourself playing something at home that you can play well and shows your ability. Remember, most bands are looking for a player who can lay down a solid groove in a variety of styles, and lock-in with the drummer. If there is a specific group for which you would like to audition, think of the kind of bassist that they may be looking for and make a tape especially for that group.

How to Prepare for an Audition

Learning to audition well can be a huge asset to your musical career. A successful band will have several bassists competing for the position. Here are some tips that could make the difference between you getting the job and someone else getting it:

TIPS

1. **Be well prepared.** When preparing for an audition, spend every spare minute learning the songs that you'll play at the audition. Play the songs over and over until you can play them in your sleep.

2. **Learn as much of the band's material as possible.** *Extra effort shows a good attitude and can be the reason that you are hired.* Show the band that if they were to hire you, you would be ready to start playing shows with only one or two rehearsals. In most cases, there will only be time for one or two rehearsals, so a successful band will need to work you in as quickly as possible.

3. **Your attitude can be as important as your playing.** The band will want to hire someone with a positive attitude, who is enthusiastic about the band and their music. When a band is looking for someone to hire, they know that they are going to be dealing with that person on a daily basis. Leave your ego at home when you are auditioning. If you are willing to relocate, be sure to tell them this. This can be a major factor in the decision of whether or not to hire you. The bottom line at an audition is that most of the time the person who gets the job is the person who wants it the most—the person with the "whatever it takes" attitude. Not all successful bands are looking for a jaded pro who has "been there, done that." A good attitude can compensate for lack of experience. Most bands are looking for members who are hungry for success. So, don't worry if you haven't played a thousand live shows or been on lots of albums. Despite your lack of experience, you could still be exactly the person they are looking for.

   Good luck!

What You May Be Asked to Play at an Audition

At most auditions, you will be asked to play some of the band's material. You may or may not be told ahead of time which songs you will play. You may be given a few minutes with a recording of a song to see how well you can learn it in a short period of time. It's likely that you'll be asked to play some of your own material as well, so have a few things prepared that you think will fit with the style of the band. The band may be interested in your songwriting style as well as your playing ability and attitude.

Equipment to Bring to an Audition

Bring a spare bass to the audition. This way, if you should happen to have problems with a string, everyone won't have to wait while you change it; you can just pick up your spare. Also bring a spare cable, an extension chord and a *ground lift* (an adapter that allows you to plug a three-prong plug into a two-prong outlet). By bringing the extension chord and ground lift, you know you'll be able to plug in your amp, which is a problem you don't want to have to deal with at the start of an audition. Change your strings the day before and make sure that all of your cables work. Before your audition, make sure that all of your equipment is in good working order. This is another way to show your professionalism.

Rehearsing and Improving the Band

Rehearsal Location

You can rehearse just about any place where you can play loudly without disturbing the neighbors. The ideal situation is one where you can leave your equipment set up and just walk in and start playing. If you can't rehearse at someone's house, check the phone book to find a rehearsal facility near you. Rehearsal facilities charge by the hour, by the day or by the month. A good way to save some money is to share the rehearsal space with another band and split the rent.

PHOTO • BOB GRUEN/COURTESY OF STAR FILE, INC.

DID YOU KNOW?

In their early days (1970), Aerosmith rehearsed in the basement of their apartment building located at 1325 Commonwealth Avenue in Boston.
In 1971, they began rehearsing at Boston's unheated Fenway Theatre, where they showcased for Frank Connoly, the agent that eventually helped them land a recording contract with Columbia Records.

Tips for Making Rehearsals More Productive

1. **Have an agenda.** Decide on the songs to be rehearsed a few days before the rehearsal. Make sure that everyone has recordings of all relevant material.

2. **Don't be afraid to stop a song if there is a problem.** Go over the problem part a few times if necessary. Make sure everyone is clear on exactly how that part should go.

3. **Don't beat a song into the ground by playing it over and over.** After playing a song more than a few times, it becomes easy to lose your focus. It is more productive to move on, even if you haven't perfected the song yet. Then, come back to it after a while. This keeps rehearsals productive and also keeps the band from burning out on a song.

4. **Record your rehearsals.** Then listen to the recording and try to find which parts need more work. Do this as a group, if possible. This can be as productive as actual rehearsal because the band can discuss how to fix any weak spots. It can be easier to hear the weak spots while listening to a recording than to hear them when the band is playing. It's also much easier to stop the recording than it is to stop the band in the middle of a song to make a comment.

5. **Be sure that all song intros and endings are solid.** The audience may or may not hear a mistake made during the song, but a mistake in the very beginning or at the very end of the song will be the most noticeable.

6. **Band Members Only at Rehearsal.** The only people who should be at a rehearsal are the members of the band. Your rehearsals will be much more productive this way, because when there is even one other person in the room, the rehearsal becomes a performance. Constructive criticism between members becomes more difficult because no one wants to be corrected or criticized in front of an audience.

People outside the band will always want to watch you rehearse. Politely tell them that your band's rehearsals are "closed." Once you have the entire show together, an open rehearsal with some invited friends can be a good opportunity to try out a live show on an audience. An open rehearsal is more of a performance than a rehearsal and should only be done when the band feels like they are ready to perform.

7. **Controlling Dynamics.** *Dynamics* refers to varying the degrees of volume. One mark of a good bassist is the ability to know when to get louder or softer. Dynamics can be controlled in several ways. One is by the use of a volume knob or pedal, and another is by how hard or soft one hits the strings. Also, the use of *palm muting* (laying the right side of your right palm gently across the strings near the bridge) is an effective way to control dynamics.

8. **A Good Way to Get Your Band Members Motivated** Book a gig. Having a show coming up will give everyone in the band something to anticipate and work toward. However, be sure that the band has enough time to prepare for it.

How Long to Rehearse Before You Play Your First Gig

Before you play your first gig, you should have rehearsed the songs until you are just starting to get bored playing them. If you know a song well enough to be bored playing it, then you know it well enough to play it live. The band will probably be somewhat nervous during its first performance. The more automatic the songs are, the less chances there are of making mistakes due to nerves.

Getting Ready for the Gig

The more prepared you are for a show, the more fun you'll have. You will be able to focus on enjoying yourself as well as focusing on what you are playing. You will always play your best when you don't have to think about what you're playing.

How to Get Gigs for Your Band

The Band's Promo Pack

In order for your band to get gigs you will need to have a promo pack. The band's promo pack should contain:

1. **A CD or tape of the band**. If your band has a CD, include one in your promo pack. If it doesn't, record three of your best songs and include the recording in your promo pack. Club owners won't want to spend a lot of time listening to your demo so three songs will be plenty.

2. **A photo of the band.** You can either get creative here or have a simple photo of the band. If you choose to get creative, be sure that the photo reflects the style of music that you play.

3. **A brief history of the band, including:**
   A. A description of the style of music that the band plays
   B. The names of the band members and what instrument they play
   C. A list of songs that the band plays
   D. A list of places that the band has played before
   E. Anything interesting about the band

4. **Any newspaper articles, reviews or press about the band.**
   Good press or reviews about the band are a great addition to a promo pack. Photocopy any articles or pictures and include the name and date of the newspaper or magazine in which they appeared.

5. **The name and number of the businessperson for the band.** For example, "for booking and information, contact John Smith at (555) 555-5555." *Be sure that this number is given in several places in the promo pack*, especially on the recording package and on the photo. In case parts of the kit get separated, they will still be able to contact you. You will need to have voicemail for your contact number so that the person who may want to book your band can leave a message. Remember that your promo pack reflects your band and its professionalism.

How to Use a Promo Pack

Give copies of your promo pack to the managers of clubs or other places that your band could play. It's also a good idea to give copies to booking agents because a good booking agent will be able to find you more gigs than you would be able to find on your own. The booking agent will charge a fee for each gig that he or she books. This may be a flat fee or a percentage of what the band is paid. You should also give copies of your promo pack to magazines and newspapers; they may want to do a review or a story on your band.

The Gig

How to Get Ready Backstage

Here's a routine that will help you warm-up and get in the right frame of mind to perform. Start with stretching until you feel limber. Then start warming up on your bass. Play chords, licks and scales, starting slowly and gradually speeding up until your hands feel loose and ready to go. Don't go overboard, though. You could fatigue your hands before the show, which defeats the purpose of warming up. You may be nervous before a performance. Deep breathing and stretching exercises can be helpful for overcoming pre-performance jitters.

Words to Keep in Mind to Help Give Your Best Performance

Instead of thinking, "let me *impress* the audience," think, "let me *entertain* the audience." Your main jobs when you're performing live are to have fun and entertain the audience. If you are having fun and are playing like there's no place you'd rather be than on stage, your audience will pick up on that attitude and enjoy watching you play.

What to Do If You Make a Mistake

There are two kinds of mistakes: arrangement mistakes and playing mistakes. An arrangement mistake is when a player forgets how the song is supposed to go and, for example, plays the wrong section of the song at the wrong time. Arrangement mistakes are usually more noticeable and are a sign that the song still needs some work. If you know your songs well, you shouldn't be making these kinds of errors.

A playing mistake is when a player plays the wrong note or chord. These mistakes are a basic part of life—even the best players make them from time to time—and are usually easy to cover up. However, if you are making more than one playing mistake every few songs, you may want to practice your parts on your own, just to refresh them.

If you make a mistake when you're performing, just relax and jump back into the song. Try not to make a face or do anything that would let the audience know that you made a mistake. Chances are, unless the mistake is really obvious, no one will even notice. Don't dwell on the mistake, just continue in the song as if it never happened. Thinking about a mistake after you make it will only distract you and cause you to make even more mistakes.

How to Make Your Mistakes Less Noticeable

It's normal to make mistakes, but one thing you can do to make your mistakes less obvious is to play right through them. The way to practice this is to pretend you are performing. Play the song from start to finish and play right through any mistakes you might make. When you are playing by yourself, you may be tempted to stop when you make a mistake. Try to resist this temptation. The golden rule of performing is this: *No matter what happens, don't stop during the song.* When you are practicing a song from start to finish, follow this rule just as you would during a performance.

Practice Playing the Songs without Looking

The less you look at your bass, the more eye contact you can have with the audience. Playing the songs without looking shows that you have confidence in what you are doing. However, there are certain times when you should look at your bass. For example, when you are shifting from one part of the fretboard to another, it is better to watch where you are going than to make the jump without looking, which could cause you to land on the wrong fret. After you practice without looking for a while, you'll start to get a feel for where the notes are on the fretboard.

PHOTO • BOB GRUEN/COURTESY OF STAR FILE, INC.

? **DID YOU KNOW?** *Bootsy Collins started out as the bassist for James Brown. In the Early 1970s , he recorded such definitive funk tracks as Sex Machine and Super Bad. He eventually founded Bootsy's Rubber Band.*

GET BETTER, SOONER

Getting Warmed Up

One of the most important parts of a practice session is the warm-up. Playing vigorously without warming up can cause injury. Just as an athlete warms up before a strenuous workout, we must warm-up our fingers before strenuous playing.

To warm up properly, all of the muscle groups you use to play should be warmed-up slowly. Different muscle groups are used to play different things. For example, we use different muscles on the fretting hand for bending strings than for playing chords. Each of these different groups of muscles must be warmed up.

The key words for warming up are *slow* and *easy*. Let your hands gradually stretch out and get your circulation going. Start slowly and gradually increase the intensity of your playing. Starting slowly has two benefits. The first is that it allows your muscles to warm-up gradually. The second is that it will keep you relaxed. Tight muscles are enemies of speed and accuracy.

Your warm-up routine could start with scales or picking exercises, then move to string bending and licks and finish with strumming. Warming up usually takes between ten and fifteen minutes but can vary depending on how often you play. The longer the periods of time between practice sessions, the longer (and slower) your warm-ups should be.

Practicing

Setting-Up Your Practice Area

The best place to practice is someplace where you won't be disturbed. Your practice area should be a place where you can get away from the rest of the world and have "your time." If you are lucky, you'll have a place where you can leave all of your materials ready to use. Even a small corner of a room will do.

What You'll Need in Your Practice Area

When you're getting ready to play, have everything that you might need within reach. This way you won't have to interrupt your train of thought just to get up and get something you need. Here are some things to keep handy in your practice area:

TIPS

1. Recording media (tapes, CDRs, whatever you use)
2. Recording device
3. Playback device (CD player, tape player, etc.)
4. Metronome or drum machine
5. Picks
6. Blank fretboard charts
7. Pencil with eraser
8. Any books or magazines that you want to work with
9. Tuner
10. Spare set of strings and a peg winder (in case you break a string)
11. Something to drink

What and How Much to Practice

When you are deciding what to practice, consider both long-term and short-term goals as a player. Your short-term goal may be to learn a song that you like or to master a new technique. Your long-term goals may range from playing for a few friends to becoming a successful recording artist. Whatever your goals are, and they may change often, try to select areas of study that will help you reach your goals. If one of your goals is to become a well-rounded player, it is important to vary your areas of study and not work on the same things during each practice session. Here is a short list of things to consider:

GIVE IT A TRY

Arpeggios
Ear training
Improvising
Learning new songs
New chords
Note naming
Phrasing

Playing songs from a
    songbook
Practicing songs that you know
Scales
Songwriting
Technique exercises
Timing and rhythm

Before you start practicing, try choosing three or four different areas that you would like to work on that day. Once you have selected them, make a list. Put them in order, starting with the area that you feel you need to focus on the most. You could even date the list, so that you can keep track of the areas you have been working on.

Keeping areas of study listed in order of priority will keep you from always playing the same things when you pick up your bass. It will also keep you focused on your goals. As you start to get bored with your work in one area, you can refer to your list and know exactly which area to focus on next.

When you finish working on the last area, go back to the first. Continue this cycle until your practice session is over. If you don't get a chance to work on all of your selected areas one day, you may want to pick up where you left off during your next practice session. Make the last area you were working on the first during the next practice session.

Make Practice a Habit

In order to improve quickly, make practice a habit. If possible, practice at the same time each day. This is important for two reasons. The first is that things are easier to start if they are a habit. This is because you don't have to plan to do them. You just do them. For example, you don't have to plan to brush your teeth at night. You just do it. If you can make picking up your bass each day as automatic as brushing your teeth, you are bound to improve more quickly. The second reason is that if you play at the same time each day, you'll get into a groove where your schedule begins to form around this time. People will begin to know to leave you alone at that time of day.

How to Tell if You're Improving

A good way to gauge your progress is to record yourself playing, write the date on the recording and then put it away for a few months. By making recordings every couple of months, you can listen back and objectively gauge your progress. Improvement comes slowly and it can be hard to tell when or how much you are improving. Ironically, the more you play, the harder it is to tell if you are improving. Just as it can be hard to notice when someone you see every day grows an inch over the course of a year, it can be difficult to notice improvement over less than a few months.

How Much You Need to Practice to be a Pro

Most professional bassists go through a time when they practice several hours a day. If you would like to make a living playing bass, plan to practice around twenty hours a week, or more. Around three hours a day is a good goal. Some days you'll have more time to play than others. But, if you want to play professionally, you'll want to make playing and practicing a high priority.

How Much Practice is Too Much

You are practicing too much when other parts of your life start to be neglected. No matter how badly you want to become a great bassist, you also need to have a life outside of the bass. Playing the bass can become an addiction. It can start to control your life instead of being a fun thing to do. Taking a day off every once in a while can actually be good for your playing.

In extreme cases, too much practice can even bring on repetitive stress injuries. If you are practicing several hours a day on a regular basis, then you need to be aware of repetitive stress injuries such as *tendonitis*. These injuries are often due to excess tension and strenuous playing without a proper warm-up.

How Often You Should Practice

The more often you practice, the faster you'll improve. Try to pick up your bass at least once a day, five or six days a week, even if you only play for a few minutes. You'll find that the more you play, the more you want to play.

Eliminating Frustration

As soon as you begin to feel yourself becoming frustrated when practicing, try taking a few slow, deep breaths. This will help relieve frustration and help you concentrate.

Usually, that feeling of frustration comes from trying to learn too much at once. You have "bitten off more than you can chew." When you feel yourself getting frustrated, slow down a little and work on a smaller amount of material (take a smaller bite). Play that smaller piece until you can play it easily, then take another small piece and do the same thing. This will give you the sense of accomplishment that makes it fun to learn new things.

Avoid Negative Thoughts

Sometimes, when you are trying to learn something new and are having difficulty, there will be a negative thought going through the back of your mind saying, "This isn't that difficult, why can't you do this yet, what's the matter with you?" Everyone has this thought at one time or another.

Do your best to ignore this thought, and remember that listening to it will do nothing but add to your frustration. Negative thoughts will make you try to learn things too quickly and may even cause you to believe that you have something learned before you do. This may cause you to move on to something new before you're ready. It takes a conscious effort to ignore these negative thoughts and go ahead and learn at a comfortable, non-frustrating pace.

When you are working on something new, listen for this kind of thought and when you hear it, realize that it is your enemy. When you can do this successfully, learning and practicing will be less frustrating, more fun and more productive.

The Importance of Review

Reviewing what you have learned is an important part of learning to play. Each new thing that you learn builds on what you have learned in the past. Reviewing makes you more able to use the things you've learned by keeping them fresh in your mind. It speeds up the learning process. It will save you from spending time re-learning things. Every month, devote a day or two of practice to review what you've learned in the past few months.

Practice Standing Up

If you are a performer or you would like to be, it is a good idea to make your practice situation as close as possible to an actual performance. If you plan to perform standing up, then you should practice standing up. Playing the bass can feel a lot different when standing and if your seated position is less than perfect, your hands may be at a different angle than when sitting down.

Why Many Short Practice Sessions are Better than a Few Long Sessions

You can learn more in a short, intense session than you can in a long, unfocused one. Your mind likes to learn things in small bits. When you're learning something new, it helps to learn in short sessions so that you can maintain a high concentration level.

Some days you will have more time to play than others. On days when time is limited, use the time to learn something new. Learn a new scale or chord, or a short, new part of a song. Then use the days when you have more time to polish the things you have learned. Repeat them until they become comfortable for you.

Getting Out Of A Rut

Every player, at one point or another, gets into a rut. We find ourselves playing the same old things each time we pick up the bass and our playing becomes stale.

The fastest way to get out of a rut is to play even more than usual. Also, try not to play any of your usual songs, licks or riffs for a week. If you tend to often play in one certain key, avoid this key completely for a week and instead play in other, less familiar keys. Each day, make it a point to learn a new song (or even part of one), or a scale or riff. Then record the new thing that you've learned and review what you've recorded the next day. Continue this until you're out of your rut.

Motivation

The best way to get motivated to play is to plan a performance. The performance can be for a few friends or family members, or a larger group of people. The desire to perform well can be extremely inspiring and tends to bring a new focus and sense of urgency to your practicing. This focus can be great for your playing, especially if you feel like your playing is in a rut.

PHOTO BY BRUCE GREGORY/COURTESY OF STAR FILE PHOTO, INC.

? DID YOU KNOW?

Sting started out as the bassist and the principle singer in the British supergroup, The Police. When The Police disbanded at the peak of their career in 1983, Sting went on to release a number of highly acclaimed solo albums.

A FEW THINGS YOU NEED TO KNOW ABOUT THE MUSIC BIZ

Getting What's Coming to You

How to Copyright a Song You've Written

Once you have written a song and recorded it on tape, you automatically own the *copyright* to that song. This means that you alone have the right to make copies of the song and sell them. In order to protect that right, it is a good idea to have your song registered with the Copyright Office of the Library of Congress. Once your song is registered, you can prove in court that the song is yours (should anyone try to steal it).

To have your song registered, you'll need to visit this Website:

http://www.copyright.gov/

Navigate to "Forms" and download the forms, or go to "Electronic Copyright Office" (eCO), where you can register online.

The Copyright Office contact information, as of this writing, is as follows:

U.S. Copyright Office
101 Independence Ave. S.E.
Washington, D.C. 20559-6000
(202) 707-3000

There is a charge each time you register, but, you can register more than one song at a time. If you register more than one song at a time, the recording you send in will need to have a name, such as "Collection of Songs."

How You Get Paid When Your Song Gets Played on the Radio

Technically, each time your song is played on the radio, on TV or anywhere else considered to be in public, you should be paid a fee. Because it would be impossible for you to keep track of each time your song is played and to collect the fee, there are agencies that do this for you. These agencies are called "performing rights collecting organizations." Their job is to monitor radio stations, TV stations and other places where songs are played for the public and pay you the fee for each time your song is played. The size of this fee depends on where your song is played. A hit song played all over the country can make the writer rich on performance royalties alone. The two main performing rights collecting organizations are ASCAP, which stands for the "American Society of Composers, Authors and Publishers" and BMI, which stands for "Broadcast Music Incorporated." To join either ASCAP or BMI, go to their Websites, or write them a letter requesting an application.

To contact ASCAP, write to: ASCAP, 1 Lincoln Plaza, New York, NY 10023 or see www.ascap.com.

To contact BMI, write to: BMI, 320 West 57th Street New York, NY 10019 or see www.bmi.com.

Why You Don't Have To Pay when Your Band Plays Another Band's Music

Club owners and promoters pay a "blanket fee" to the performing rights collecting organizations. This fee covers all of the performance royalties for the music performed in their venue.

Career Tips

Where You Should Live
To become a pro, it will help to live in or near a major music city. Some cities that are known for their music scene are: New York, NY; Los Angeles, CA; Nashville, TN; and Austin, TX. There are many cases of bands making it out of small towns, but most successful bands are based in cities with thriving music scenes. There are several reasons for this. One is that major music cities have more places for bands to play. Another is that most music industry companies are in major cities.

Networking and How it Can Help Your Career
Networking is the process of making contacts within the music industry. To a certain extent, the old saying, "it's not what you know but who you know" can be true. Who you know can play a large part in your success as a musician. Well-connected people have made a science out of networking. They know that the people who are on their way up are the people who make the best contacts.

Keep an eye out for energetic, ambitious people who are moving up in the industry. These are the people who will end up in high positions later on. You never know where someone will end up. A person interning at a record label could someday be the president of that label. The person who will be the most likely to help your career is a person that you have known for some time. The ideal contact is one who you knew when they were first starting out and have kept in touch with over time.

Getting a Record Contract
There are several different ways to get a record contract. To understand how to get a record contract, it will help to understand how a record company works.

A record company is basically a bank that lends artists money and is paid back through record sales. After the record company *recoups* (makes back all of the money that they spent on recording, promotion and tour support) the remaining money made from record sales is divided between the record company and the band.

The person at the record company that "signs" a band is called an "A&R" person (artists and relations). The A&R people take a big chance when they sign a band because they could end up losing their job if the band is not successful.

One way to get a record contract is to record an album yourself, sell as many copies as possible and build up a following by playing live and promoting your band. A record company is more likely to sign a band that has already proven itself by building up a fan base and selling albums on its own.

Another way to get a record deal is to make a demo of a few of your band's best songs and send it to an A&R person at a record company. If the A&R person hears the demo and thinks your band just may be the next big thing, he or she will want to see the band play live. The catch here is that the A&R person is unlikely to take the time to listen to your demo, unless they have already heard about your band from a trusted source.

The way to get them to listen to your demo is to be recommended by an inside source. For more information on the music business, check out the book *This Business of Music: The Definitive Guide to the Music Industry,* by M. William Krasilovsky, et al.

Performance Contract

Here is a sample contract for a private party or wedding gig. You can use this as a template to create your own contract, adding or subtracting points as necessary. Anywhere you see text underlines, just replace it with your own information.

(Your name, address, phone number, fax number and e-mail address here)

Dear John Doe,

This contract will confirm our engagement to provide music for your wedding reception to be held on June 17 in the year 2010 beginning at 7:00 p.m. We will play the equivalent of 3 sets of 50 minutes each between the hours of 7:00 p.m. and 10:00 p.m. with two short breaks of 10 minutes each, during which we will provide recorded music. Our attire will be suits and our repertoire will consist of see attached list. The band consists of Steven Jones, keyboards; Bill Smith, guitar; John Brown, bass; Thomas Miller, percussion.

As agreed, I will provide the following equipment: all musical equipment, PA system, recorded music during breaks.

You will provide the following equipment: sheltered playing area, electrical power.

Food and drink of the same quality provided to your guests will also be provided for the band *[note here whether the band is to be fed free of charge, are subject to a cash bar, etc.]*. It is to be made clear to the caterer and/or staff at the venue that the band members are to be treated as your guests. *[These items are pertinent mainly if you are playing a gig at which is food is to be served. Note that if your band consists of more than eight people, it may be difficult to get the client to agree to a "free food" arrangement.]*

Our fee for this engagement will be $800.00, which includes all transportation costs. To activate this agreement I must receive a nonrefundable deposit of $80.00 by June 3, 2010. The balance is to be paid to me immediately following the engagement. If overtime is required, and if other obligations do not prevent us from continuing our performance, the rate is $150.00 per half hour, or any fragment thereof.

In case of injury or illness, at my sole discretion I reserve the right to replace any member of my group to ensure the quality of performance you have requested. Please make sure that we are advised of any special song requests well in advance. If you have more than one special request, additional rehearsal costs will apply. Also, please make sure to provide us with adequate directions to the engagement at least two (2) weeks in advance.

Please sign and immediately return both copies of this agreement to me along with the deposit. I will countersign and immediately send one copy to you for your files. If the deposit is in the form of a check, please make it payable to Steven Jones.

If you should have any further questions, feel free to contact me via the information above.

Sincerely,
Steven Jones

Accepted by (X) _____ dated February 1, 2010

Address_____

Telephone _____ Email_____

True Stories

Here are a couple of true stories about bands that have gotten signed to major labels.

Dirty Looks

Dirty Looks was a band that played the club circuit and had a few independent albums out on a small record label from France called Axe Killer Records. The band built up a strong following by playing constantly up and down the East Coast. They changed record companies and released an album on Mirror Records, which belonged to the owner of a large music store in Rochester, New York called the "House of Guitars." This album was reviewed in Billboard Magazine and the next day several record companies, including Atlantic Records, contacted them and were interested in hearing the band. The next few months were spent showcasing for different labels and the band eventually decided to sign with Atlantic Records.

PHOTO: RD TOWNSEND (1987)

FROM LEFT TO RIGHT:
Paul Lidel, the author
Henrik Ostergaard
Gene Barnett
Jack Pyers

Dangerous Toys

Dangerous Toys was signed to Columbia Records after a friend sent a tape of the band playing live to a manager she knew in Los Angeles. The tape sat on the manager's desk for two months. When he finally listened to it, he contacted the band immediately and arranged to fly to Austin, Texas to see them play. The band signed a contract with the manager that said the manager had ninety days to get the band a record contract. The manager knew people at Columbia Records and arranged for an A&R person from the label to see the band play live. Soon after this performance, the band was signed to Columbia Records.

PHOTO: WYATT MCSPADDEN (1994)

CLOCKWISE FROM BOTTOM:
Jason McMaster
Mark Geary
Paul Lidel, the author
Scott Dalhover
Mike Watson

PART 5: REFERENCE

STRINGS

There are many reasons why different types of bass guitar strings sound different. Strings come in various *gauges* or thicknesses. Thinner strings are often easier for beginners to play and have a brighter sound, while thicker strings tend to have a beefier tone. There are three main types of *windings* for bass guitar strings: *round-wound*, *flat-wound*, and *half-flat*. Each type has its own distinctive feel and sound. Round-wound strings feel somewhat rough under your fingers, due to the many windings. They have the brightest, most aggressive sound, but are prone to finger noise as you move your hand around. Flat-wound strings have the windings flattened so that they feel smooth and do not generate as much finger noise. They have a deep, mellow sound. Half-flat strings are a compromise between the two.

Changing the Strings

After much playing, strings wear out and sound "dead." Although bass strings are thicker than normal guitar strings, they do break, and it's always a good idea to have a spare set of strings around. Following are instructions for changing a string on the bass. If you are changing all the strings, follow these directions for each string.

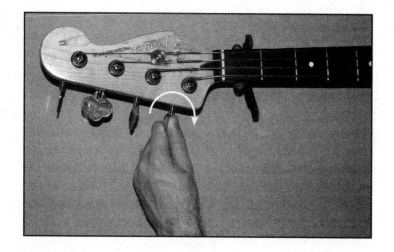

1. Loosen the string by turning the tuning machine clockwise (there are rare occasions where a bass may have reverse-thread tuning machines, and you will need to tune the opposite direction).

2. Pull the string through the bridge.

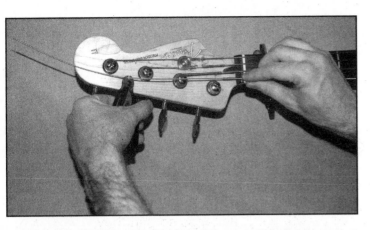

3. Insert the new string through the bridge, pull tightly across neck, and cut off any excess string about two inches past that string's tuning machine.

4. Insert the string in the string post and twist it around the post in a clockwise fashion.

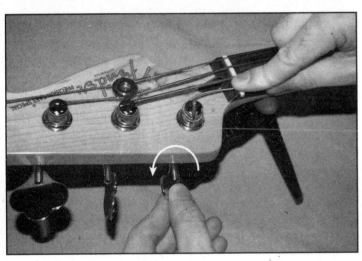

5. Then, turn the tuning machine counter-clockwise and tune up that string.

Stretching the Strings

New strings will always go out of tune much more easily than older strings, and the reason for this is that the older strings have been stretched over time from playing and tuning.

A way to avoid having to constantly tune your new strings is to stretch them once they are on your bass. An effective way to do this is to first tune all the strings to the correct pitch. Then, take one string, pull it out as far as it can go, and let it snap back into place (see right); do this about three times and then re-tune that string. Repeat this process until the stretching no longer causes the string to go out of tune. Do this with all of your strings, and you will find that your bass stays in tune much longer.

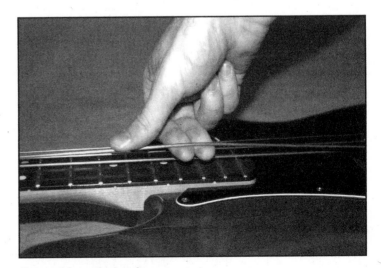

Stretching the strings.

BASS FINGERBOARD CHART

The Bass Notes in the First Octave

The following chart shows the position of every bass note in the first octave (the first 12 frets)

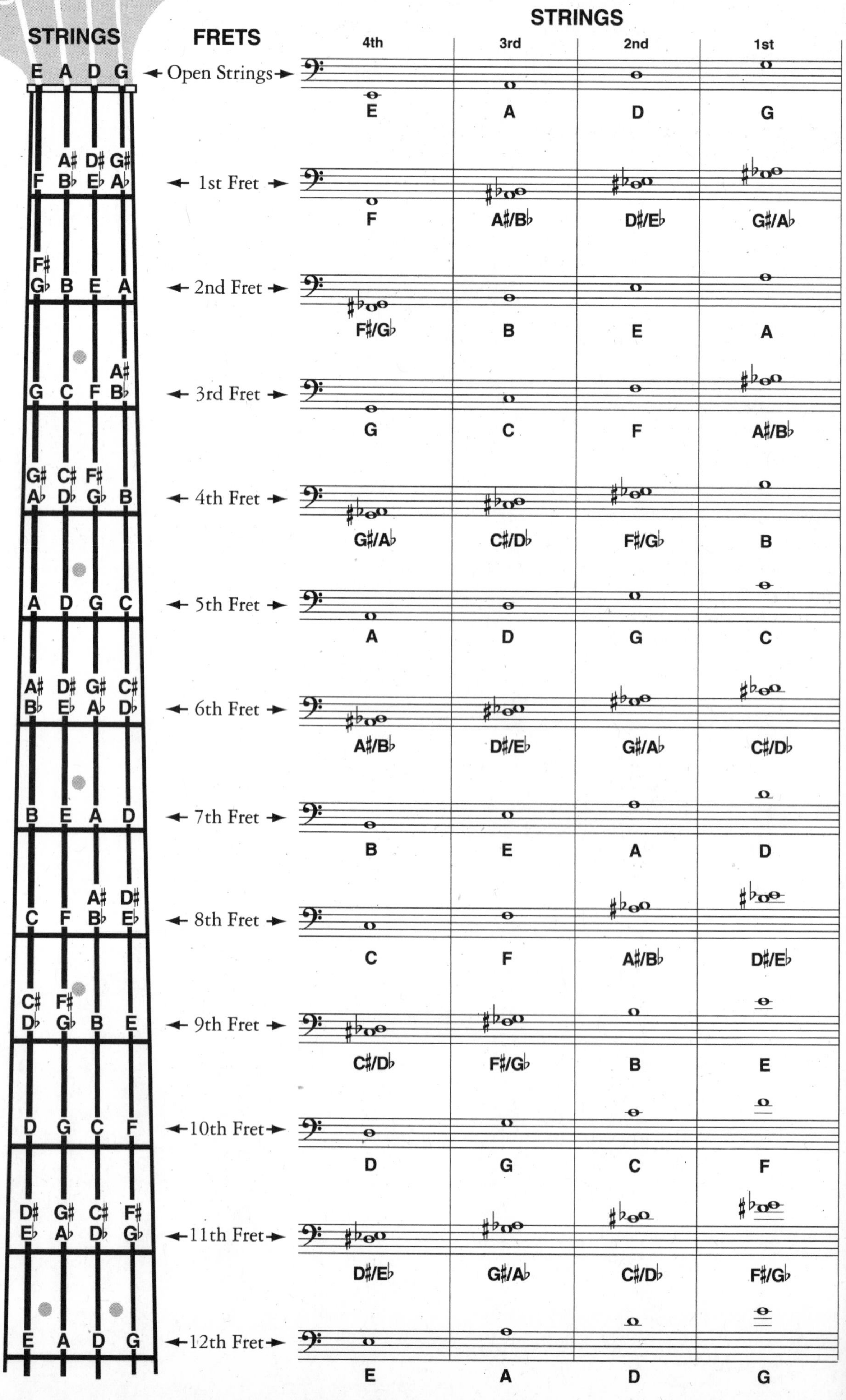

SCALES AND MODES

Learning scales and modes and being able to identify their sounds will give you a better command of the fretboard. This approach to learning and organizing melodic material will greatly enhance your bass prowess.

What Are Scales and Modes?

A *scale* is a set of notes with a particular arrangement of whole and half steps. Each scale has a different sound because of its unique arrangement of these intervals.

Modes are scales derived from the major and minor scales.

How to Use This Section

Each scale and mode is presented with two parts. The first part describes the scale or mode, lists chords that work well with it and the musical styles in which it is most commonly used, and shows the intervals of the scale or mode. The second part shows the scale or mode in several (usually five) different positions on the neck. The positions are shown using a neck diagram, in standard music notation, and in tablature.

All scales and modes are given in the tonality of E to show how they relate to one another. Using the various positions, you can play these scales anywhere on the neck and in any key. In each neck diagram, a note with a square around it is the *root* or *tonic* note, which, in this book, will always be E. To put these scales into other keys, simply take the root note and move it, using the note chart below, to the root of the key in which you wish to play.

Note Chart

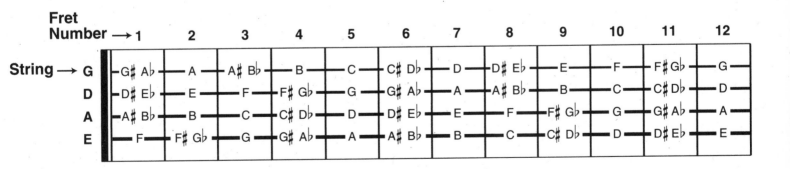

Major Scale

Description
This scale is used as the basis from which many scales and modes are derived. This scale has a happy, upbeat, almost jubilant quality.

Chords
Major, Major Seventh, Major Ninth, Eleventh

Musical Styles
Rock, Pop, Country, Jazz, Fusion

E Major Scale

Intervals

Root		2		3		4		5		6		7		Octave
	W		W		H		W		W		W		H	

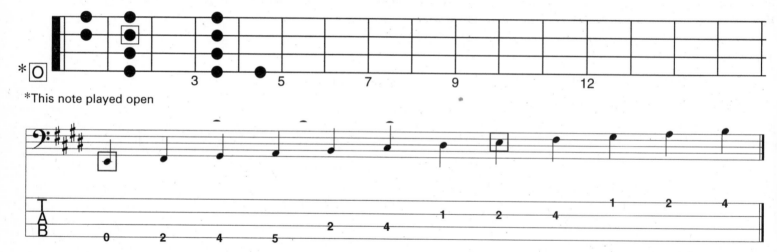

*This note played open

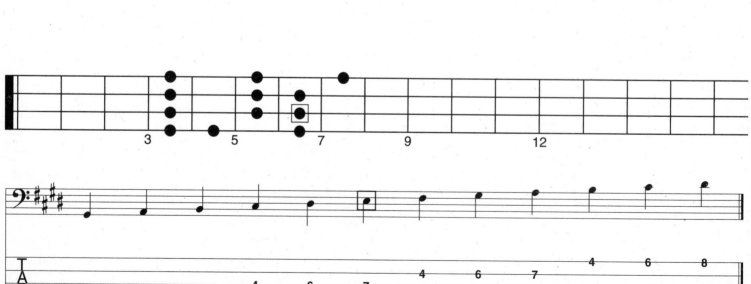

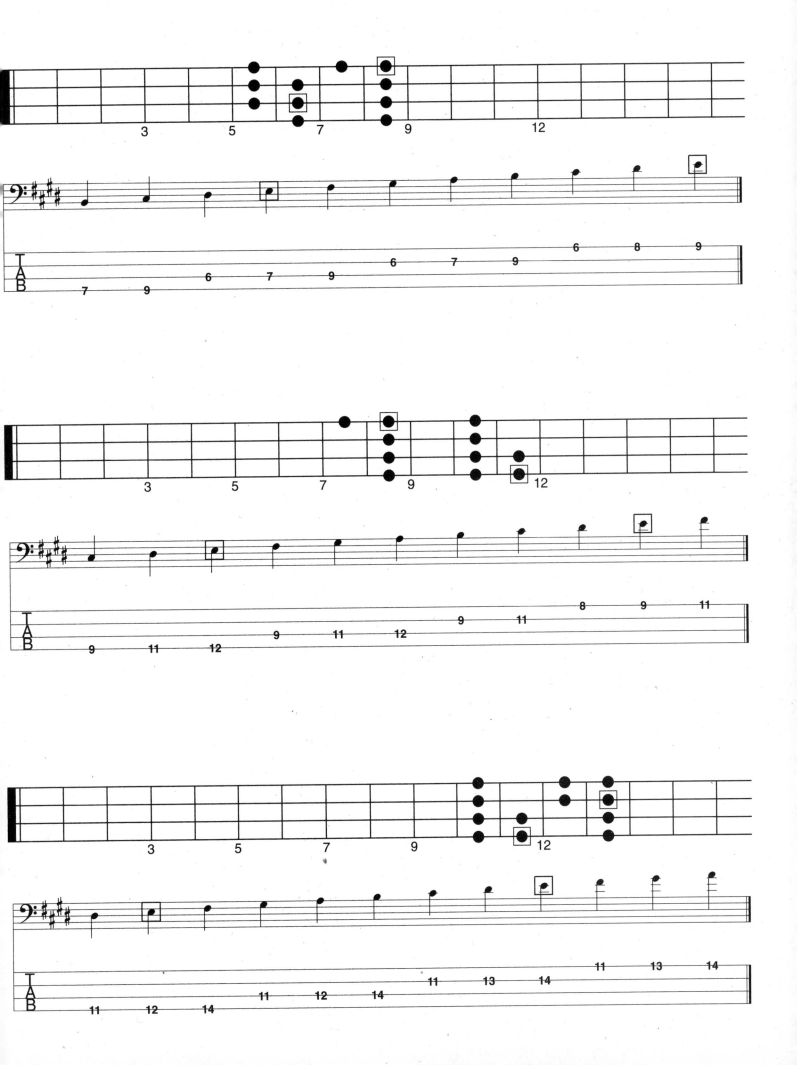

Dorian Mode

Description
This is the major scale with the third note and seventh note lowered 1/2 step. This jazz flavored mode has a sophisticated, soulful sound.

Chords
Minor, Minor Seventh, Minor Ninth

E Dorian Mode

Musical Styles
Jazz, Fusion, Blues, Rock

Intervals

Root	2	♭3	4	5	6	♭7	Octave
	W	H	W	W	W	H	W

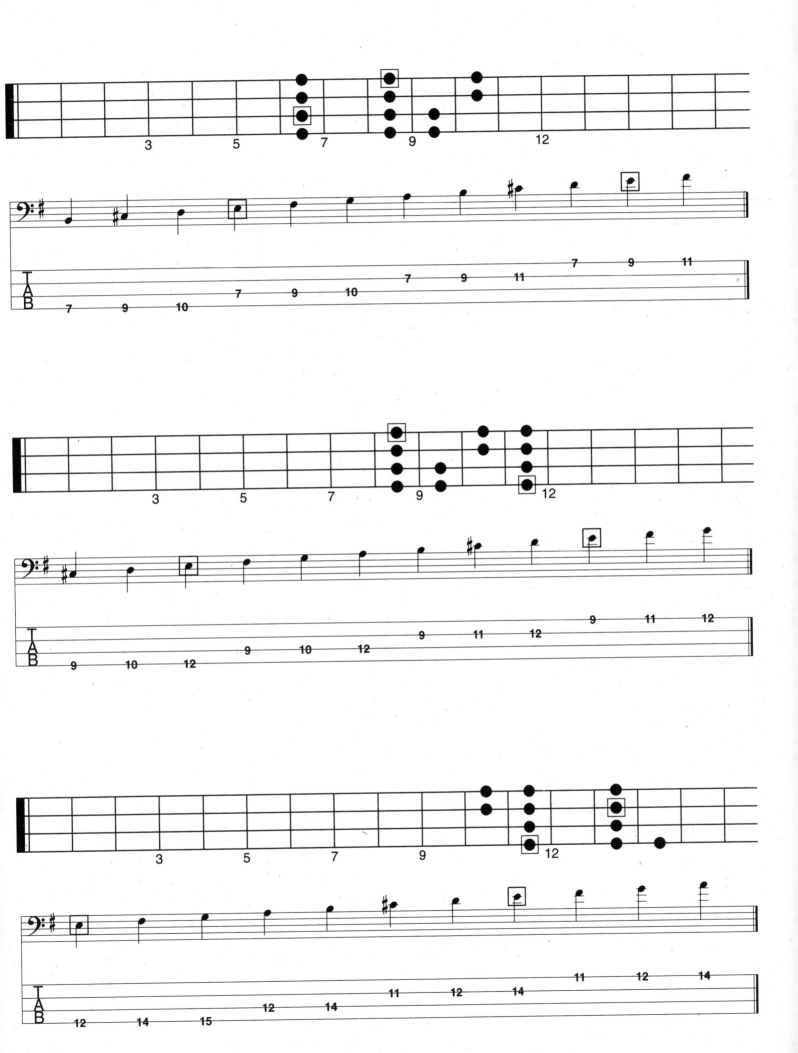

PHRYGIAN MODE

Description

This is the major scale with the second note, third note, sixth note and seventh note lowered 1/2 step. It is most commonly thought of as the flamenco mode, for its Spanish flavor. It is also often used by fusion and, strangely enough, speed metal players.

Chords

Major, Minor, Minor Seventh

Musical Styles

Flamenco, Fusion, Speed Metal

E Phrygian Mode

Intervals

Root	♭2	♭3	4	5	♭6	♭7	Octave
	H	W	W	W	H	W	W

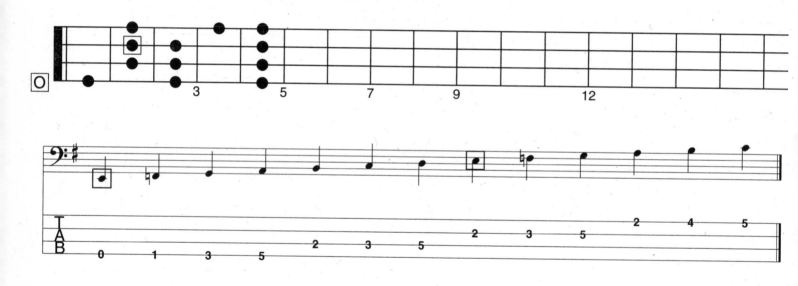

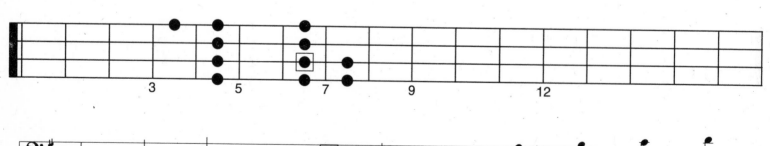

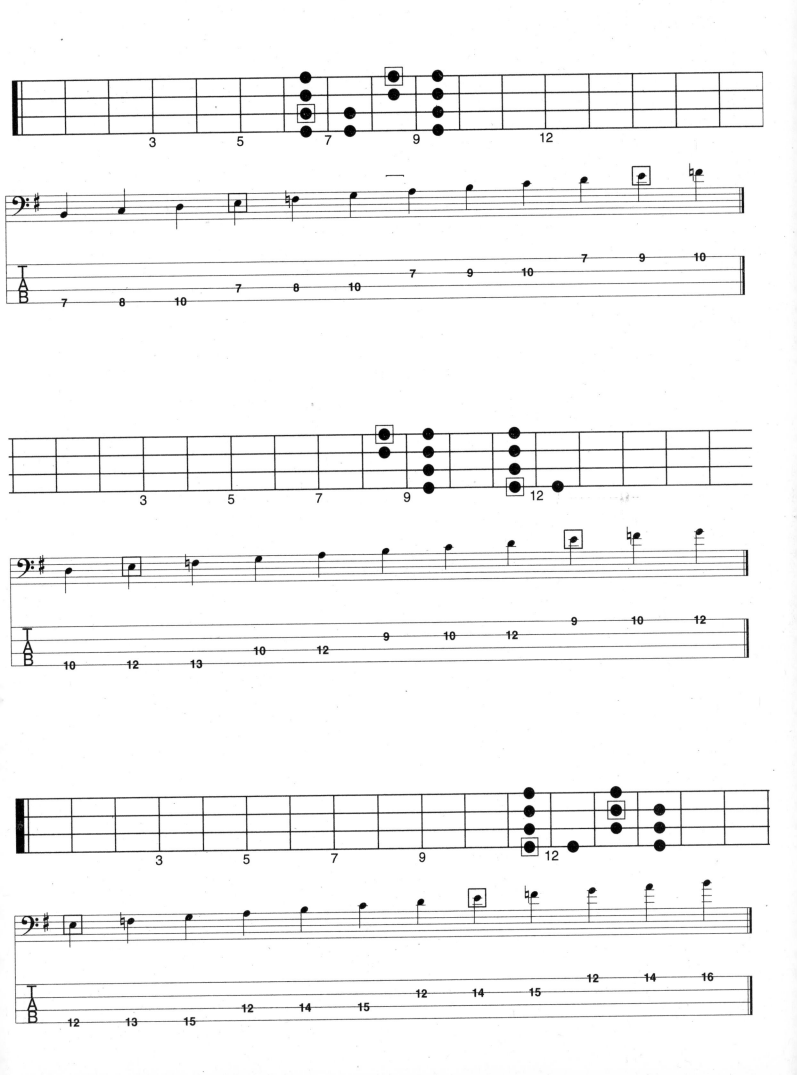

Lydian Mode

Description
This is the major scale with the fourth note raised 1/2 step. This gives the scale an airy sound favored by the likes of Stu Hamm and John Pattituci.

Chords
Major, Major Seventh, Major Ninth, Sharp Eleventh

E Lydian Mode

Musical Styles
Jazz, Fusion, Rock, Country

Intervals

Root	2	3	♯4	5	6	7	Octave
	W	W	W	H	W	W	H

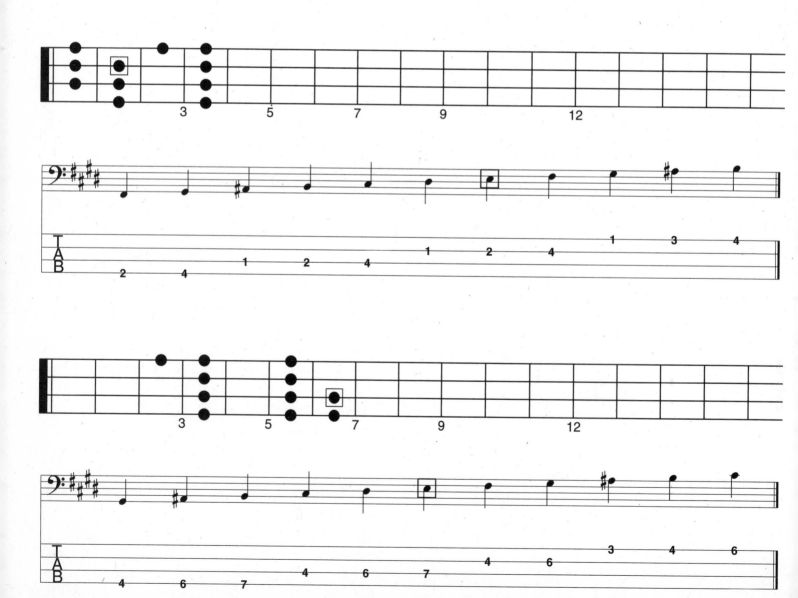

Mixolydian Mode

Description
This is the major scale with the seventh note lowered 1/2 step. This mode has a blues feel that also lends itself well to country and rockabilly.

Chords
Dominant Seventh, Dominant Ninth

Musical Styles
Blues, Country, Rockabilly, Rock

E Mixolydian Mode

Intervals

Root	2	3	4	5	6	♭7	Octave
	W	W	H	W	W	H	W

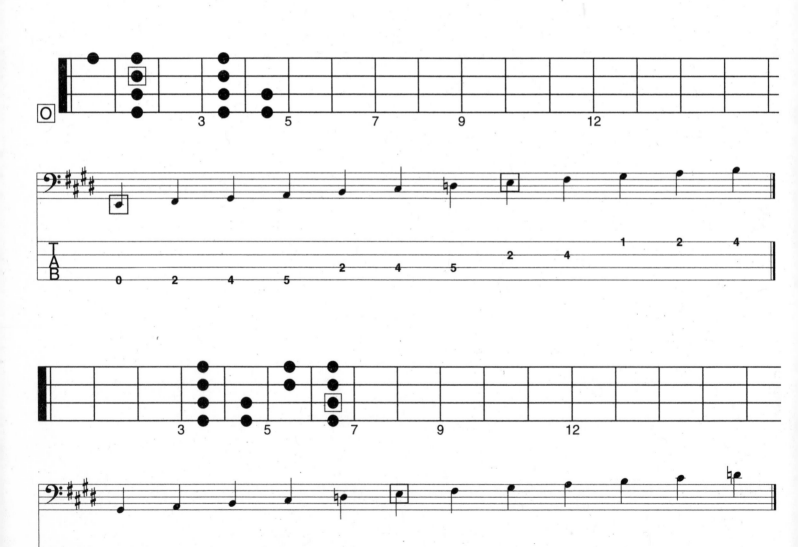

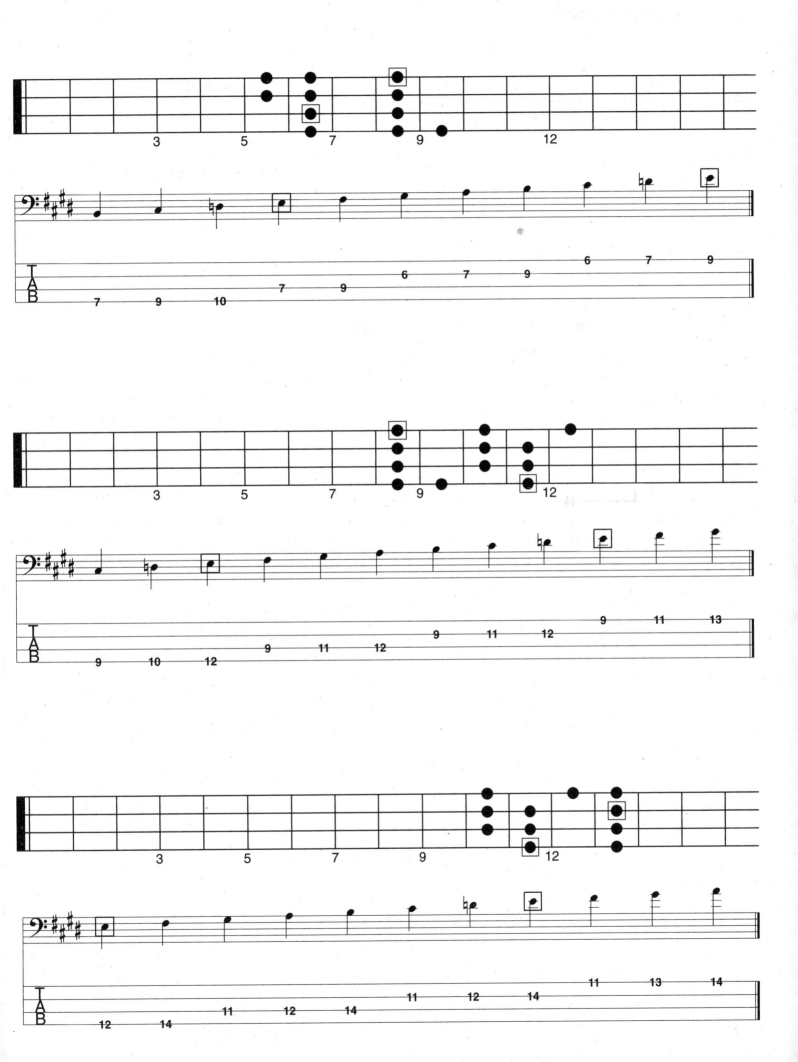

Locrian Mode

Description
This is the major scale with the second note, third note, fifth note, sixth note and seventh note lowered 1/2 step. This mode has a sinister sound that is mostly used by jazz players.

Chords
Minor Seventh Flat Five

E Locrian Mode

Musical Styles
Jazz, Fusion

Intervals

Root	♭2	♭3	4	♭5	♭6	♭7	Octave
H	W	W	H	W	W	W

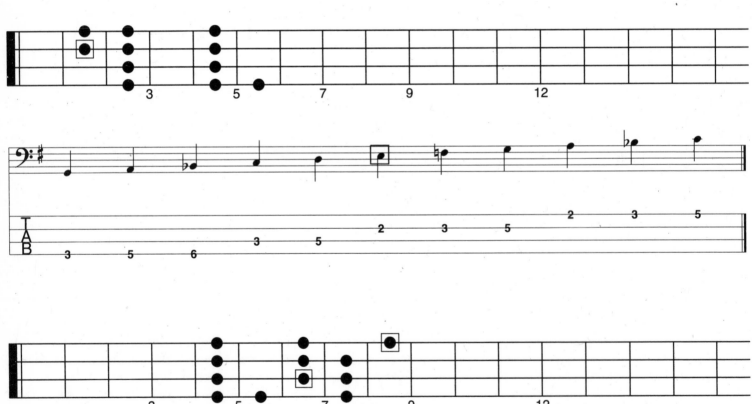

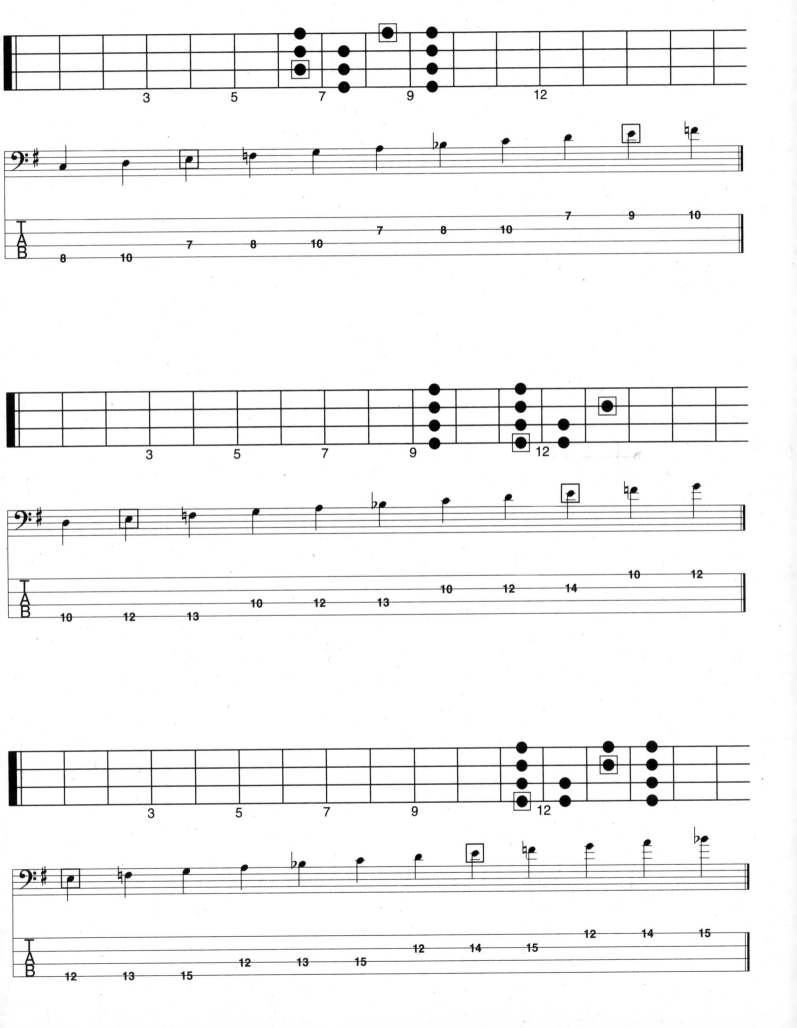

Natural Minor Scale

Description
This is the saddest of all scales, and is used in many different styles of music to express sorrow and pain. It is also known as the Aeolian mode, and is one of the most often used scales in Western music.

Chords
Minor, Minor Seventh, Minor Ninth

E Natural Minor Scale

Musical Styles
Pop, Blues, Rock, Heavy Metal, Country, Fusion

Intervals

Root	2	♭3	4	5	♭6	♭7	Octave
	W	H	W	W	H	W	W

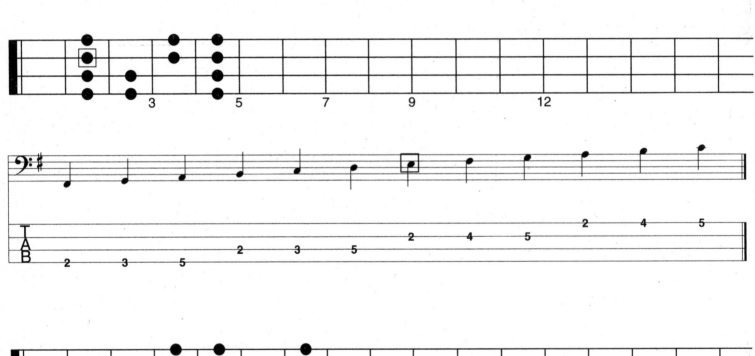

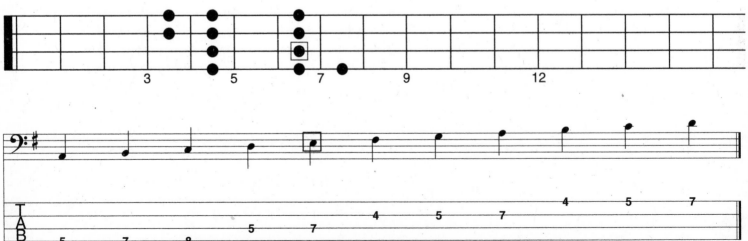

Harmonic Minor Scale

Description
This scale has an unusual sound that is very popular in classical music, most particularly the
Baroque period. It is favored by classically influenced rock and heavy metal musicians.

Chords
Minor, Minor (Major Seventh), Major Fifth (Power Chord)

E Harmonic Minor Scale

Musical Styles
Classical, Rock, Heavy Metal, Jazz

Intervals
Root   2   ♭3   4   5   ♭6   7   Octave

     W   H   W   W   H   W+H   H

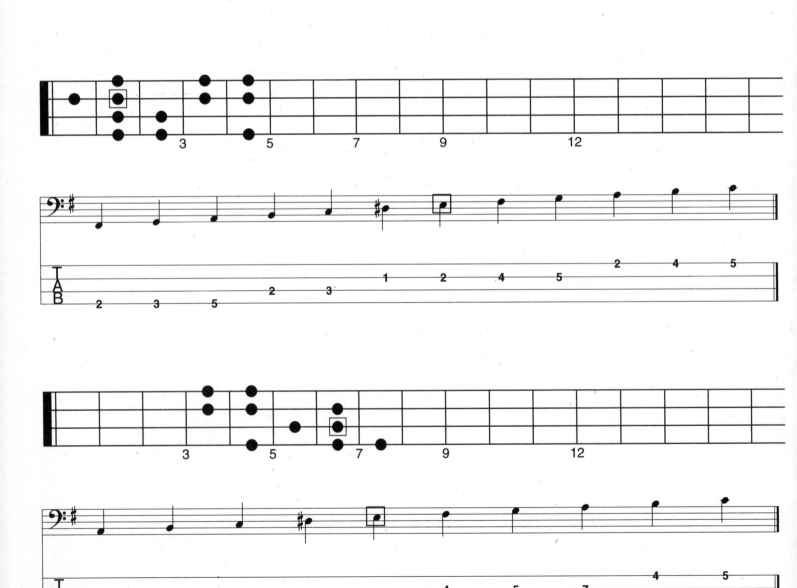

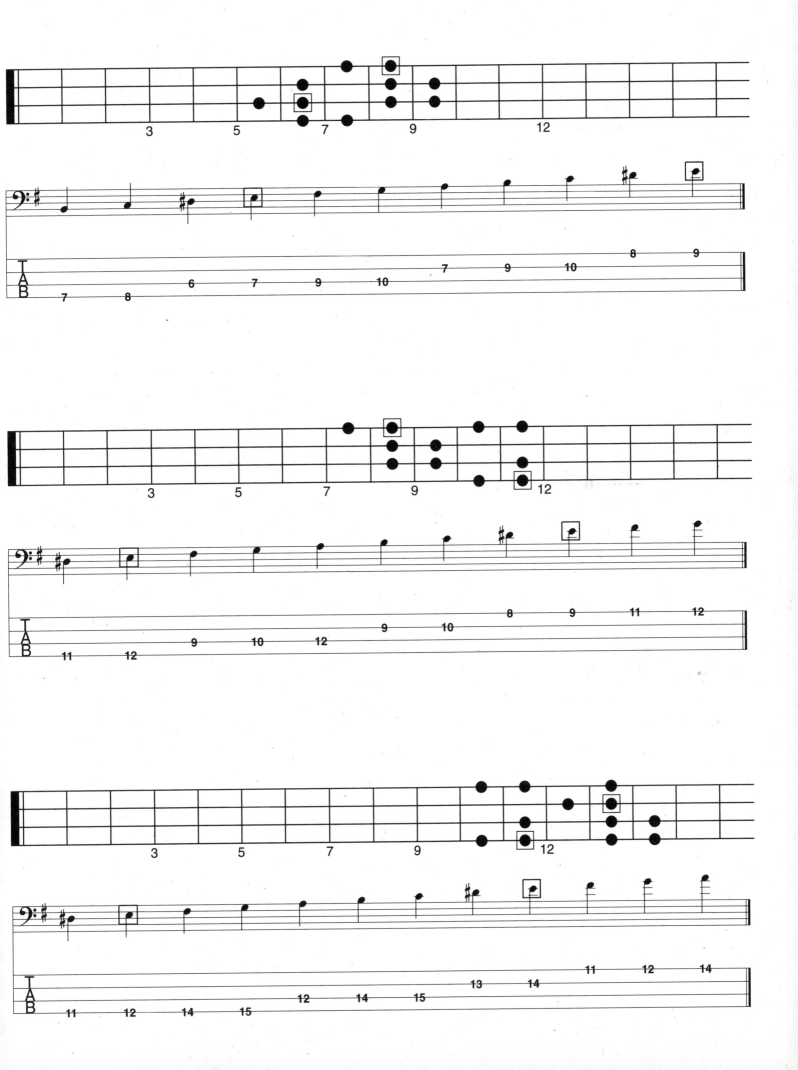

Melodic Minor Scale

Description
This is commonly known as the jazz minor scale. It is very useful in that it has qualities of both major and minor scales which express a wide range of emotions.

Chords
Minor, Minor (Major Seventh), Minor Sixth

Musical Styles
Jazz

E Melodic Minor Scale

Intervals

Root	2	♭3	4	5	6	7	Octave
	W	H	W	W	W	W	H

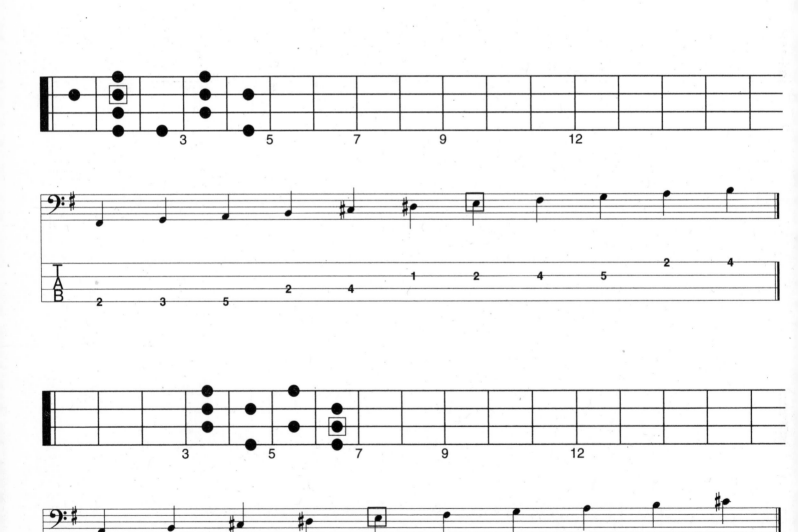

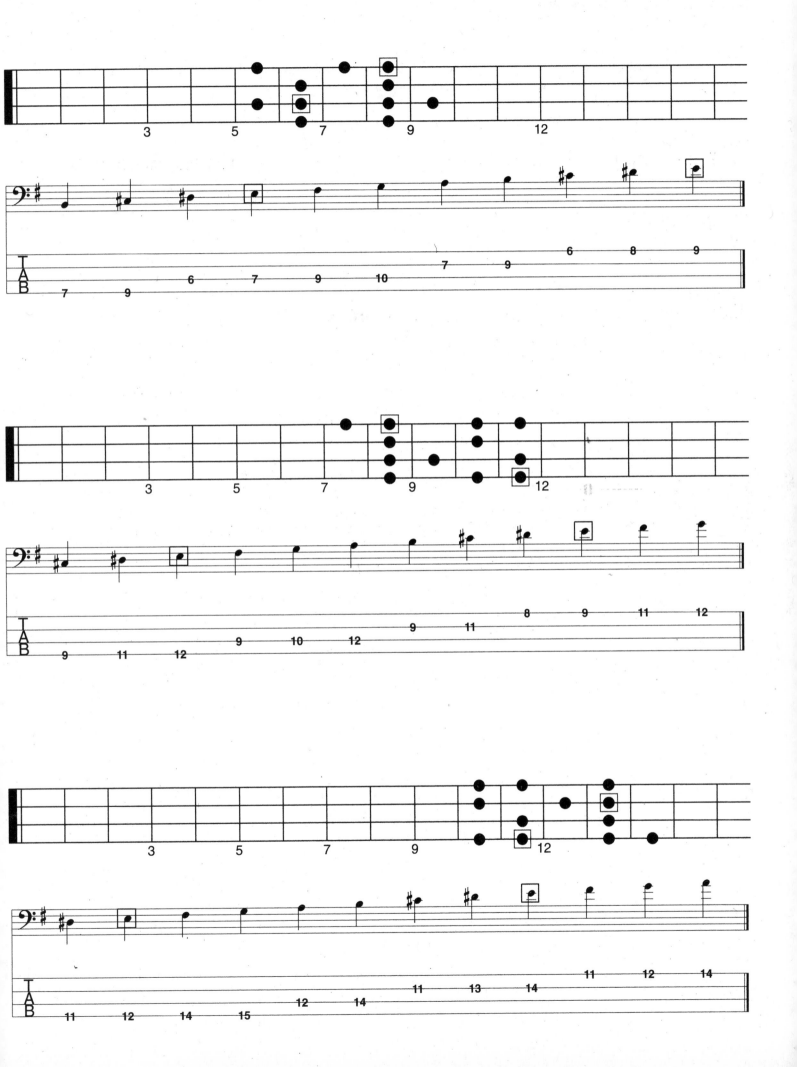

Whole Tone Scale

Description
This is a scale constructed of tones a whole step apart, which keeps it from being anchored to any pitch. This lack of tonal center gives the scale a dreamlike floating quality.

Chords
Dominant Seventh Flat Five, Augmented

Musical Styles
Jazz, Fusion, Contemporary Classical

E Whole Tone Scale

Intervals

Root	2	3	#4	#5	b7	Octave
	W	W	W	W	W	W

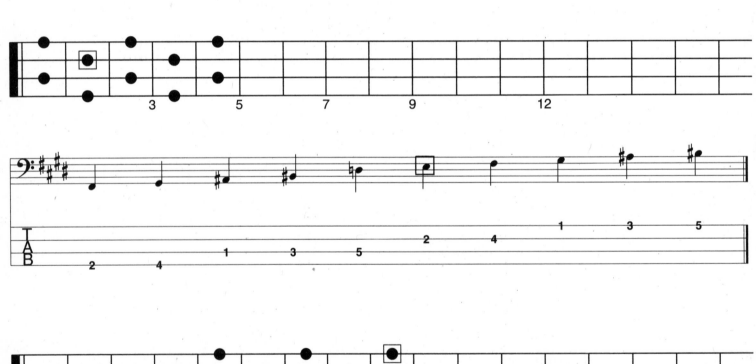

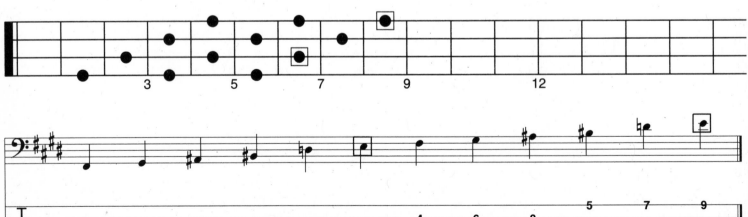

Diminished Scale

Description
This is an important jazz scale because it works well with altered seventh chords and chord extensions popular in this style of music. In heavy metal it is used over the flat five power chord which gives it an almost Gothic sound.

Chords
Diminished Seventh, Minor Seventh Flat Five, Dominant Seventh Flat Nine

E Diminished Scale

Musical Styles
Jazz, Fusion, Heavy Metal, Blues

Intervals

Root	2	♭3	4	♭5	♭6	♮6	7	Octave
W	H	W	H	W	H	W	H	

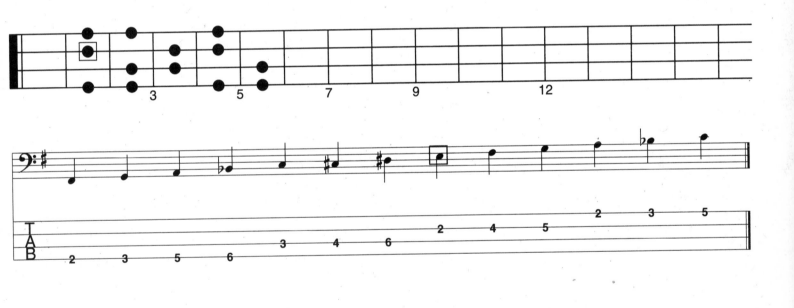

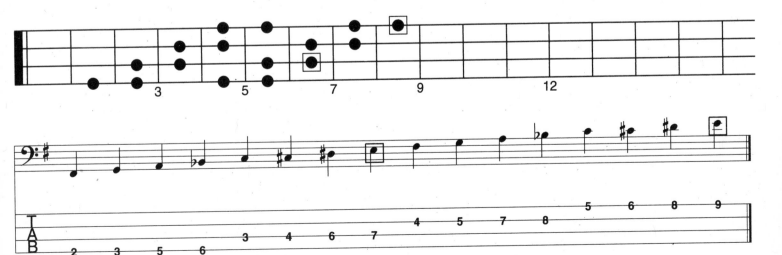

Major Pentatonic Scale

Description
The pentatonic scale dates back thousands of years, and is still one of the most used today. The major pentatonic has a bright sound which lends itself well to country music.

Chords
Major, Major Seventh, Dominant Seventh

E Major Pentatonic Scale

Musical Styles
Country, Blues, Fusion, Jazz, Rock

Intervals

Root	2	3	5	6	Octave
	W	W	W+H	W	W+H

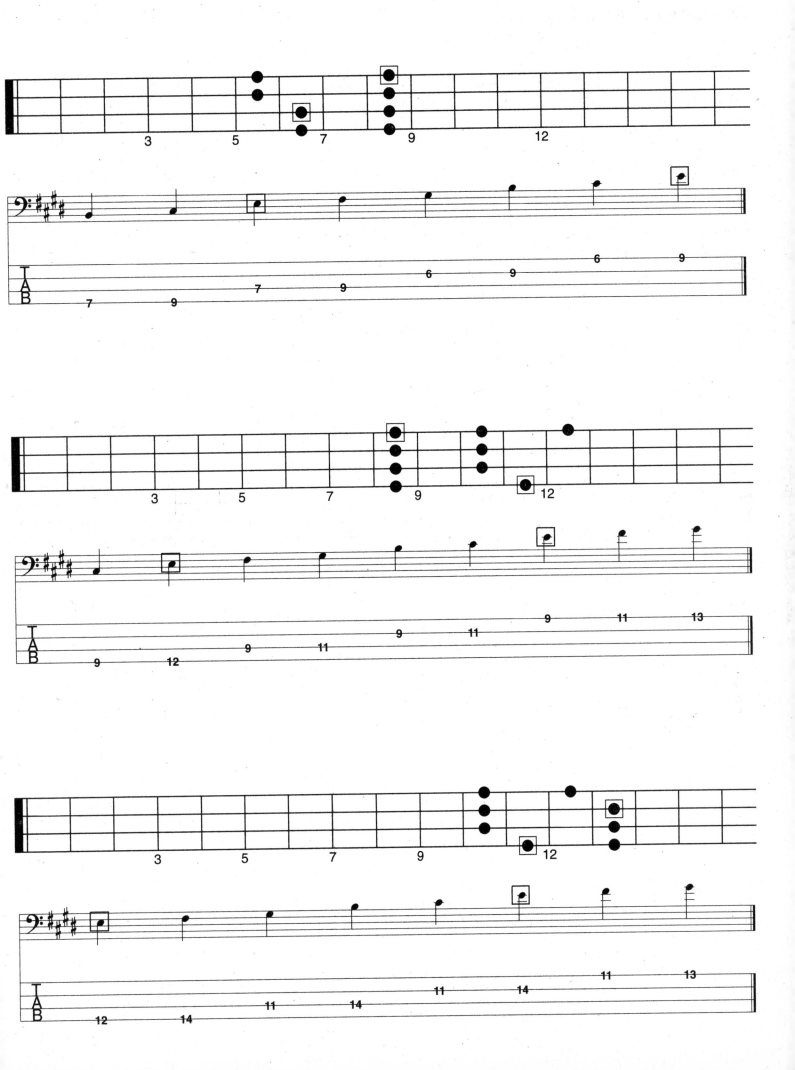

Minor Pentatonic Scale

Description
This bluesy sounding scale is by far the most used in blues and rock. One of the reasons for this is because when played over most common blues and rock chord progressions, this scale leaves a small margin for error.

Chords
Minor, Minor Seventh, Dominant Seventh

E Minor Pentatonic Scale

Musical Styles
Rock, Blues, Heavy Metal, Fusion, Jazz

Intervals
Root   ♭**3**   **4**   **5**   ♭**7**   **Octave**

     W+H   **W**   **W**   **W+H**   **W**

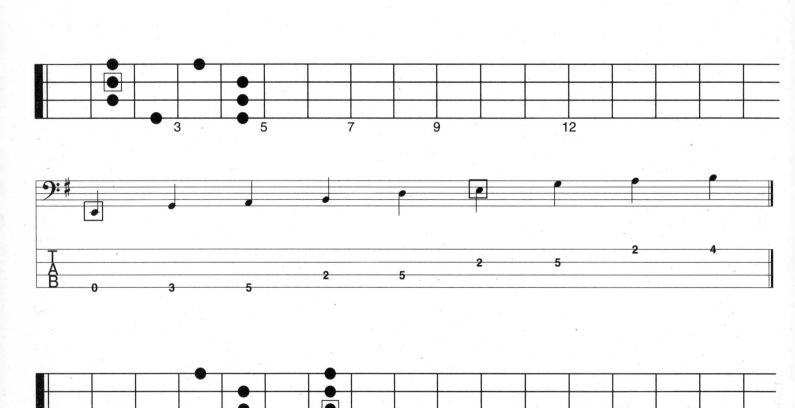

Blues Scale

Description
This is the minor pentatonic with the addition of one note, the raised fourth, which gives it a uniquely blues sound.

Chords
Major Fifth, Dominant Seventh, Dominant Ninth,
Minor Seventh, Minor Ninth

E Blues Scale

Musical Styles
Blues, Rock, Jazz, Fusion

Intervals
Root	♭3	4	♯4	5	♭7	Octave
	W+H	W	H	H	W+H	W

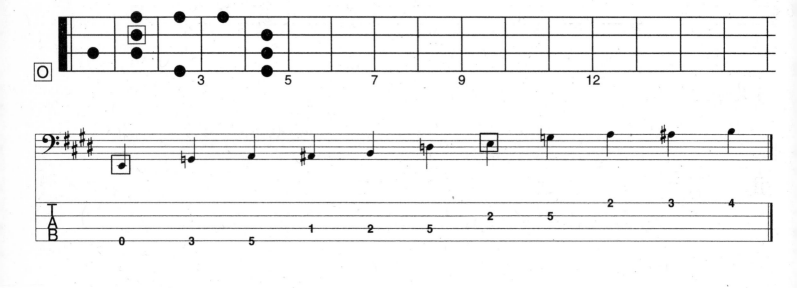

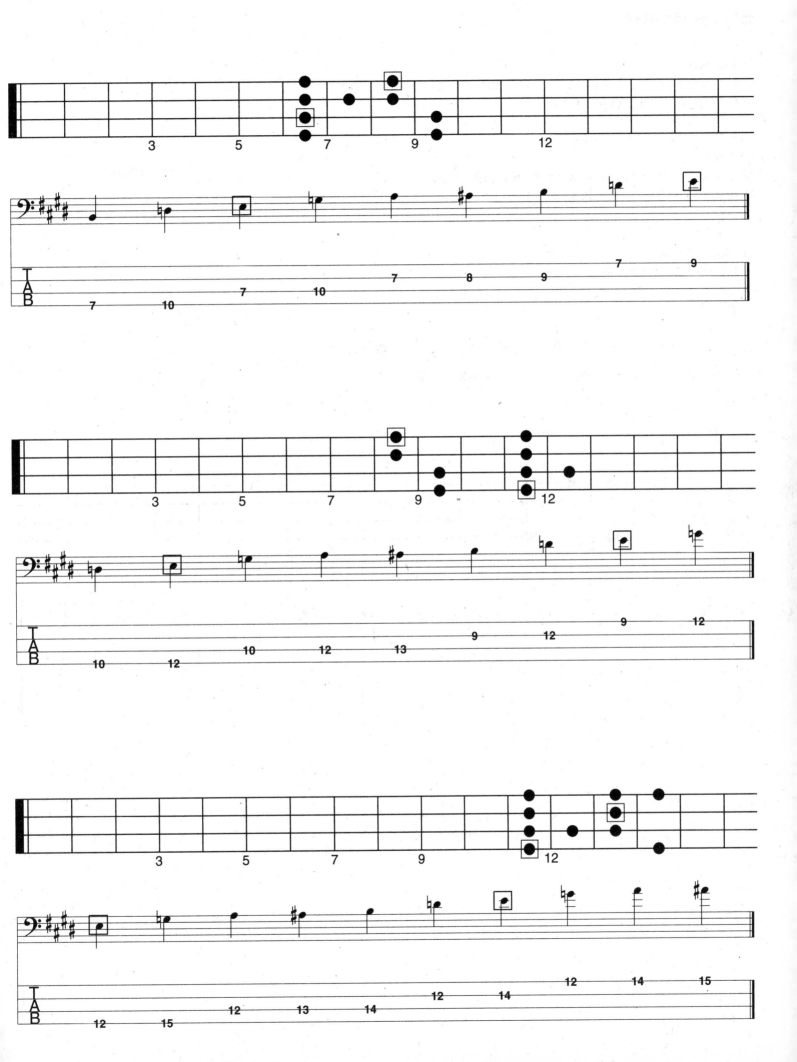

BASS CHORDS

A thorough understanding of chords and the ability to voice and execute those chords in the appropriate situations is essential. Whether it is a simple chord on the last beat of a song, a power chord groove or a seventh chord in the right spot, chords can be the perfect complement to a great bass line. This section is designed to help you expand the possibilities of your bass playing through the understanding of chords and the fingerings needed to play them. Knowledge of standard music notation and bass guitar technique will help you get the most out of this part of the book, which is divided into two parts:

- **Part 1: Theory** (page 217) provides the basics of music theory, including how chords are built and used in different keys.

- **Part 2: The Chords** (page 219) is where you will find fingerings for all the chords covered in this book. We start with all the A chords and work our way to G and finally A♭, (remember, A♭ is the same as G♯. You find the following chord types for each key: 5 (power chord, e.g. A5), major (A), minor (Am), diminished (A°), augment (A+), seventh (A⁷), major seventh (Amaj⁷), and minor seventh (Am⁷). This is just the tip of the chord iceberg, and it is highly recommended that you pick up a good chord resource, such as *The Bass Chord Encyclopedia* by Tracy Walton.

While the traditional role of a bass player still remains to lay down the groove, if you stay true to yourself and the needs of a song, chords can be a great tool to express yourself. Enjoy.

FRETBOARD DIAGRAMS

To get started, you need to be able to read fretboard diagrams. To the right is an example with the parts labelled.

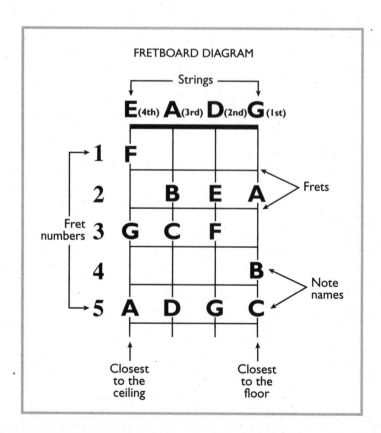

Chord Theory

Two notes played together are referred to as an interval or a *double stop.* Three or more notes played at the same time make a *chord.*

Triads

A *triad* is a three-note chord. Each triad in this section will be analyzed in three ways: 1) through its intervals above the *root* (the lowest note and namesake of the triad); 2) how it relates to a major scale; 3) and as stacked 3rds.

Ⓡ = Root

Major Triad

A *major triad* consists of a root, a major 3rd and a perfect 5th. A major triad can also be built from the 1st, 3rd and 5th scale degrees of a major scale. Finally, a major triad can be built by stacking two 3rds: a major 3rd under a minor 3rd. For example, a C Major triad has a major 3rd from C to E and a minor 3rd from E to G. The symbol for a major triad is just the note name. C Major is "C."

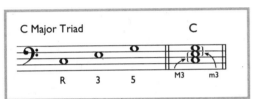

Major Triad Fingering

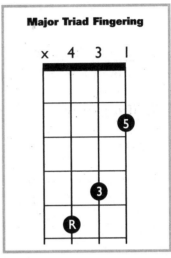

Minor Triad

A *minor triad* consists of a root, a minor 3rd and a perfect 5th. A minor triad can also be built from the 1st, ♭3rd and 5th scale degrees of a major scale. Finally, it can be thought of as a minor 3rd under a major 3rd. The symbols commonly used for a C Minor triad are Cmin, Cm or C-. In this book, it is Cm.

Minor Triad Fingering

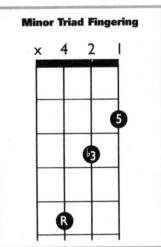

Diminished Triad

A *diminished triad* consists of a root, a minor 3rd and a diminished 5th. A diminished triad can also be built from the 1st, ♭3rd and ♭5th scale degrees of a major scale. Finally, a diminished triad can be thought of as two stacked minor 3rds. The symbols commonly used for a C Diminished triad are Cdim or C°. In this book, it is C°.

Diminished Triad

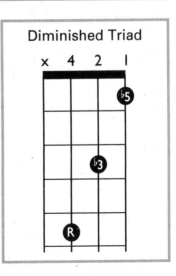

Augmented Triad

The *augmented triad* consists of a root, a major 3rd and an augmented 5th. An augmented triad can also be built from the 1st, 3rd and ♯5th scale degrees of a major scale. Finally an augmented triad can be thought of as two stacked major 3rds. The first chord of "Oh! Darling" by the Beatles is an augmented triad.

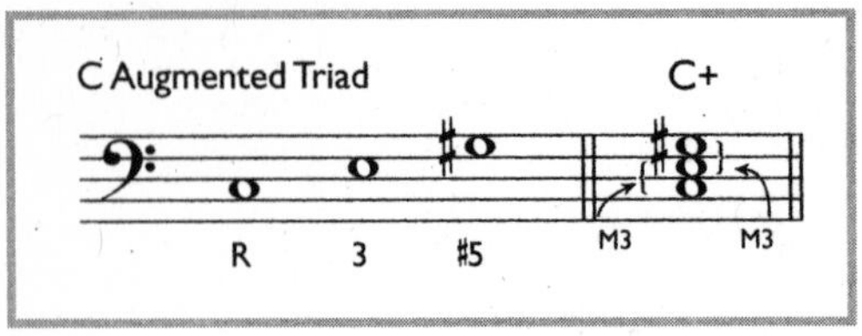

Augmented Triad Fingering

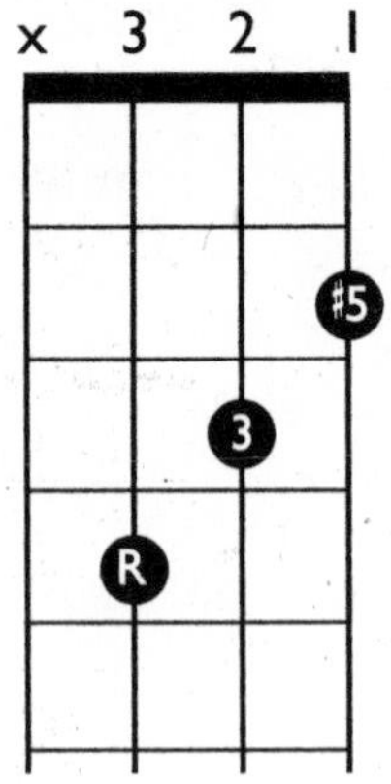

Below is a summary of triads.

Triad	**Scale Degrees**	**Intervals Above the Root**	**Stacked 3rds**
Major	1–3–5	Root, M3, P5	M3, m3
Minor	1–♭3–5	Root, m3, P5	m3, M3
Diminished	1–♭3–♭5	Root, m3, d5	m3, m3
Augmented	1–3–♯5	Root, M3, A5	M3, M3

Diatonic Triads in Major Keys

Each major key has seven *diatonic* triads. Diatonic means "belonging to the key." The diatonic triads for each key are found by building a triad from each of the seven scale degrees of a major scale.

To build diatonic triads in a major key, start with the seven notes of the given key. Then add a 3rd and 5th above each scale degree. Be sure that each 3rd and 5th are members of that major scale. This is called *harmonizing the scale.* Let's use the key of C Major as an example.

First, spell a C Major scale.

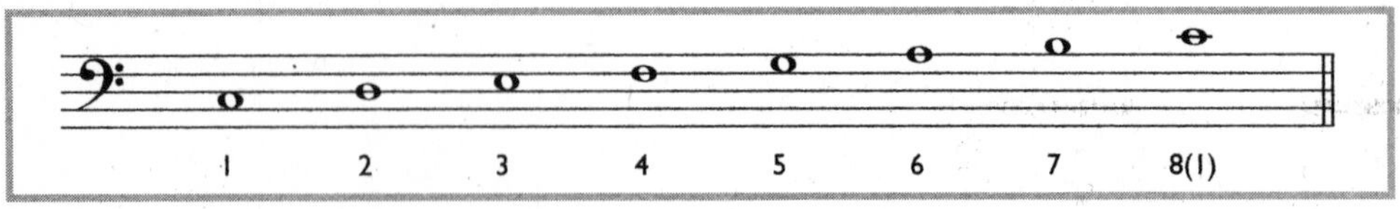

Next, build a triad using the 3rd and 5th above each scale degree. Notice that every triad consists of every other note of the major scale above that root. Finally, check the quality of each triad to see if it is major, minor or diminished (there is no augmented triad in a major key).

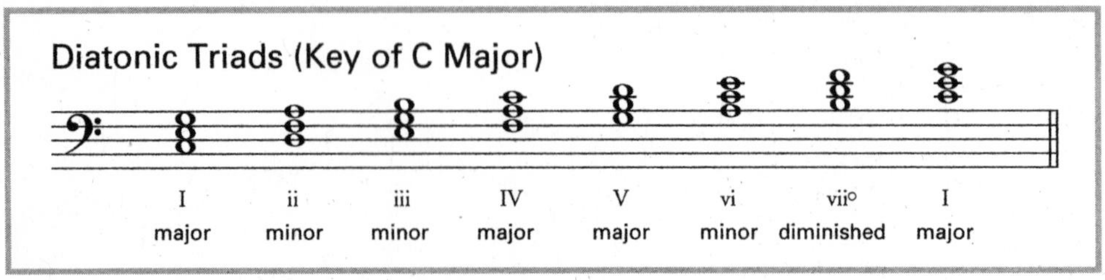

This is sometimes called a *chord scale.*

Because each major scale is built using the same whole-step/half-step formula, the qualities of the diatonic triads will remain consistent for every key. For this reason, Roman numerals are used to analyze the triads in a given key. The Roman numerals agree with the number of the scale step. There is a quick review of Roman numerals and their Arabic equivalents to the right.

Roman Numeral Review

I or i.......... 1	V or v.......... 5
II or ii.......... 2	VI or vi.......... 6
III or iii.......... 3	VII or vii.......... 7
IV or iv.......... 4	

Basic Chord Dictionary

A

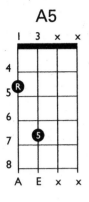
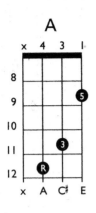
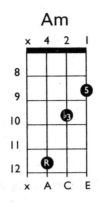
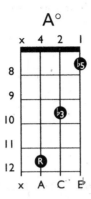

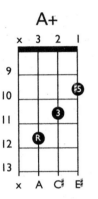
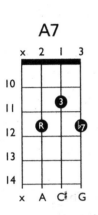
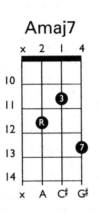
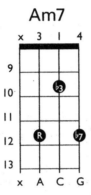

B♭ (A♯)

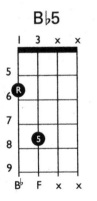
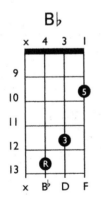
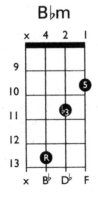
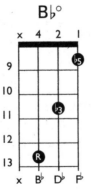

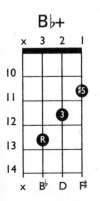
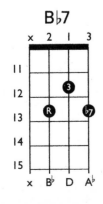
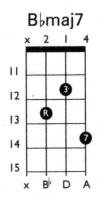
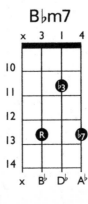

220

B

B5
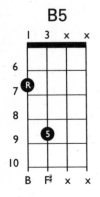

B
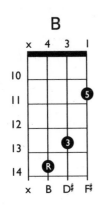

Bm
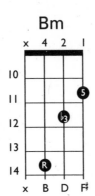

B°
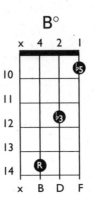

B+
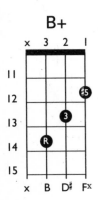

B7
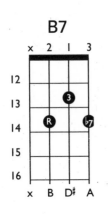

Bmaj7
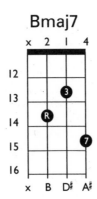

Bm7
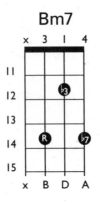

C

C5
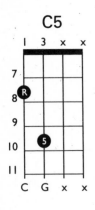

C
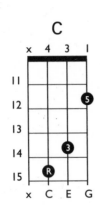

Cm
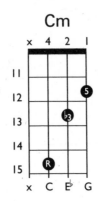

C°
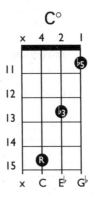

C+
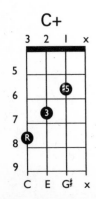

C7
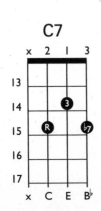

Cmaj7
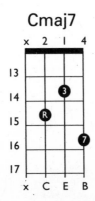

Cm7
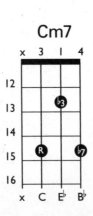

D♭(C♯)

D♭5
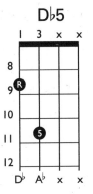

D♭
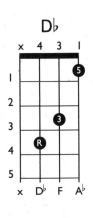

D♭m
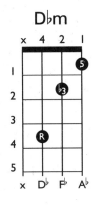

D♭°

D♭+
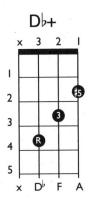

D♭7
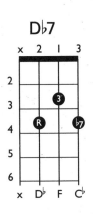

D♭maj7
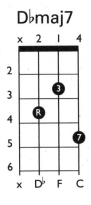

D♭m7
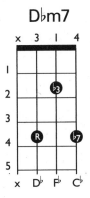

D

D5
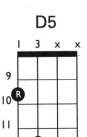

D
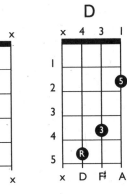

Dm
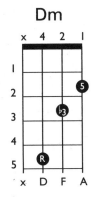

D°
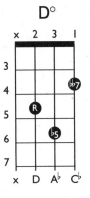

D+
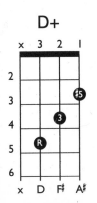

D7
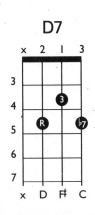

Dmaj7
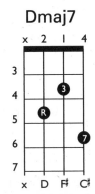

Dm7
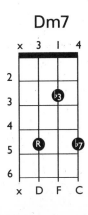

E♭(D♯)

E♭5
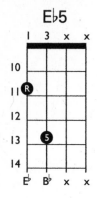

E♭
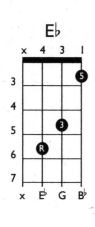

E♭m
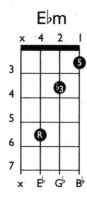

E♭°
(image)

E♭+
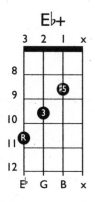

E♭7
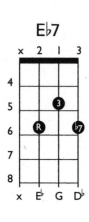

E♭maj7
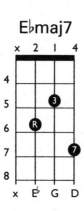

E♭m7
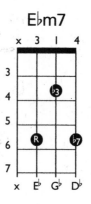

E

E5
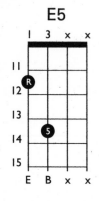

E
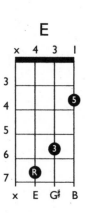

Em
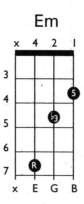

E°
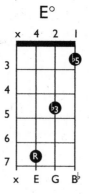

E+
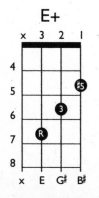

E7
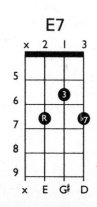

Emaj7
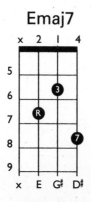

Em7
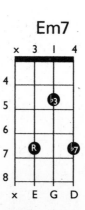

E

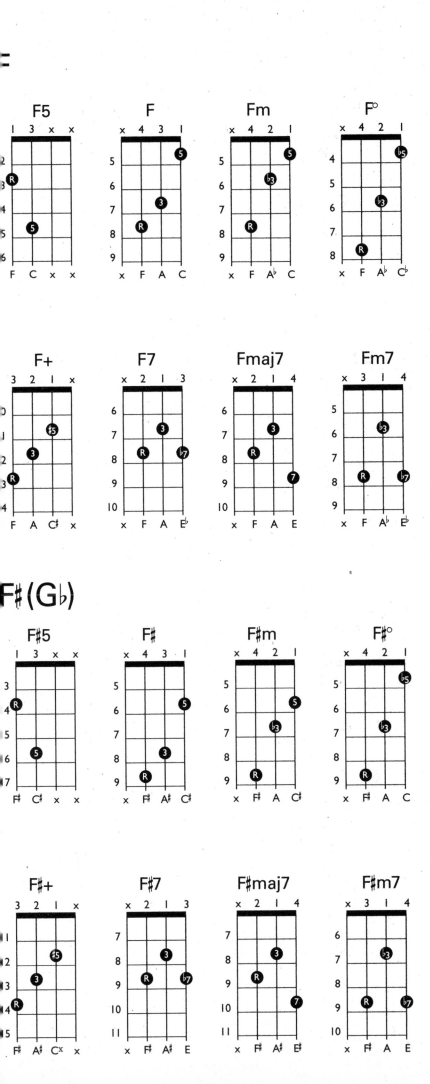

F5
1 3 x x
F C x x

F
x 4 3 1
x F A C

Fm
x 4 2 1
x F A♭ C

F°
x 4 2 1
x F A♭ C♭

F+
3 2 1 x
F A C♯ x

F7
x 2 1 3
x F A E♭

Fmaj7
x 2 1 4
x F A E

Fm7
x 3 1 4
x F A♭ E♭

F♯ (G♭)

F♯5
1 3 x x
F♯ C♯ x x

F♯
x 4 3 1
x F♯ A♯ C♯

F♯m
x 4 2 1
x F♯ A C♯

F♯°
x 4 2 1
x F♯ A C

F♯+
3 2 1 x
F♯ A♯ Cx x

F♯7
x 2 1 3
x F♯ A♯ E

F♯maj7
x 2 1 4
x F♯ A♯ E♯

F♯m7
x 3 1 4
x F♯ A E

G

G5
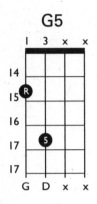

G
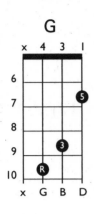

Gm
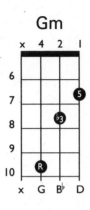

G°
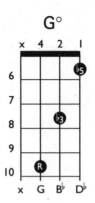

G+
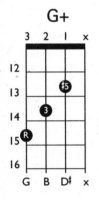

G7
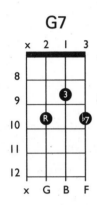

Gmaj7
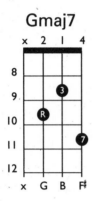

Gm7
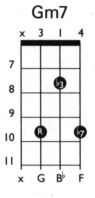

A♭(G♯)

A♭5
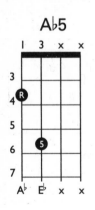

A♭
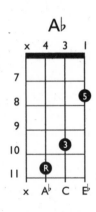

A♭m
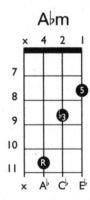

A♭°
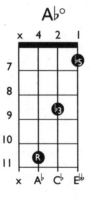

A♭+
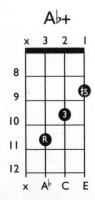

A♭7
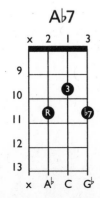

A♭maj7
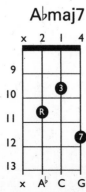

A♭m7
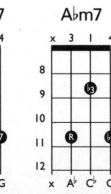